ROUTLEDGE LIBRARY EDITIONS: LIBRARY AND INFORMATION SCIENCE

Volume 68

PRICING AND COSTS OF MONOGRAPHS AND SERIALS

PRICING AND COSTS OF MONOGRAPHS AND SERIALS
National and International Issues

Edited by
SUL H. LEE

LONDON AND NEW YORK

First published in 1987 by The Haworth Press, Inc.

This edition first published in 2020
by Routledge
2 Park Square, Milton Park, Abingdon, Oxon OX14 4RN

and by Routledge
52 Vanderbilt Avenue, New York, NY 10017

Routledge is an imprint of the Taylor & Francis Group, an informa business

© 1987 The Haworth Press, Inc.

All rights reserved. No part of this book may be reprinted or reproduced or utilised in any form or by any electronic, mechanical, or other means, now known or hereafter invented, including photocopying and recording, or in any information storage or retrieval system, without permission in writing from the publishers.

Trademark notice: Product or corporate names may be trademarks or registered trademarks, and are used only for identification and explanation without intent to infringe.

British Library Cataloguing in Publication Data
A catalogue record for this book is available from the British Library

ISBN: 978-0-367-34616-4 (Set)
ISBN: 978-0-429-34352-0 (Set) (ebk)
ISBN: 978-0-367-40983-8 (Volume 68) (hbk)
ISBN: 978-0-367-40986-9 (Volume 68) (pbk)
ISBN: 978-0-367-81033-7 (Volume 68) (ebk)

Publisher's Note
The publisher has gone to great lengths to ensure the quality of this reprint but points out that some imperfections in the original copies may be apparent.

Disclaimer
The publisher has made every effort to trace copyright holders and would welcome correspondence from those they have been unable to trace.

Pricing and Costs of Monographs and Serials: National and International Issues

Sul H. Lee
Editor

The Haworth Press
New York • London

Pricing and Costs of Monographs and Serials: National and International Issues is monographic supplement #1 to *Journal of Library Administration*, Volume 8, 1987. It is not supplied as part of the subscription to the journal, but is available from the publisher at an additional charge.

© 1987 by The Haworth Press, Inc. All rights reserved. No part of this work may be reproduced or utilized in any form or by any means, electronic or mechanical, including photocopying, microfilm and recording, or by any information storage and retrieval system, without permission from the publisher. Printed in the United States of America.

The Haworth Press, Inc., 12 West 32 Street, New York, NY 10001
EUROSPAN/Haworth, 3 Henrietta Street, London WC2E 8LU England

Library of Congress Cataloging-in-Publication Data

Pricing and costs of monographs and serials.

"Monographic supplement #1 to Journal of library administration, volume 8, 1987" — T.p. verso.
Bibliography: p.
1. Acquisitions (Libraries) — Congresses. 2. Library materials — Prices — Congresses. 3. Books — Prices — Congresses. 4. Serial publications — Prices — Congresses. 5. Libraries and publishing — Congresses. 6. Library finance — Congresses. I. Lee, Sul H. II. Journal of library administration ; v. 8 (Supplement #1)
Z689.P882   1987   025.2'1   86-33653
ISBN 0-86656-620-1

For Melissa

CONTENTS

Introduction   ix
   Sul H. Lee

Pricing From Three Perspectives: The Publisher, the Wholesaler, the Library   1
   Kent Hendrickson

The Approval Connection: Pricing the Ordering Alternatives   13
   Jennifer Cargill

   External Factors   14
   Collection Development Factors   16
   Internal Acquisitions and Processing Factors   19
   Technology   22
   Summary   22

Truth in Vending   27
   Leonard Schrift

Books Across the Waters: An Examination of United Kingdom Monographic Pricing   37
   Dana Alessi

Mountains and Molehills: How University Presses Determine Book Prices and How Those Prices Relate to Library Budgets   47
   George W. Bauer

Acquisitions Costs: How the Selection of a Purchasing Source Affects the Cost of Processing Materials   53
   Edna Laughrey

   Ordering   54
   Pre-Coding   54
   Inputting   57
   Mailing   59
   Receiving   59
   Payment   61
   The Choice   64
   Conclusion   64

Differential Pricing of Monographs and Serials   67
    Christian M. Boissonnas

The Cost of Global Serials: The Vendor's Perspective   79
    Kit Kennedy

    Common Vocabulary: Standardization   79
    The Cooperative Framework: Users, Suppliers, Sources   80
    Global Serials   81
    Place of Publication   82
    The Vendor's Perspective on Serial Cost   84
    Conclusions   86

The Library's Cost and the Vendor's Price for Serials   89
    James T. Stephens

    Library Cost Considerations   91
    Publisher Pricing   92
    Subscription Agency Pricing   94
    Summary   96

Materials Costs and Collection Development in Academic Libraries   97
    Lenore Clark

    Compensating   98
    Cost-Cutting   99
    Communication   101
    Consumerism   102
    Collection Management   104
    Coordinated Collection Development   107
    Conclusion   108

Introduction

On February 20 and 21, 1986, the University of Oklahoma Libraries and the University of Oklahoma Foundation sponsored a national conference on the pricing and costs of monographs and serials. Ten papers were presented by a panel of librarians and vendor executives. The conference registrants included librarians and vendors representing twenty states and Canada.

Librarians in the 1980s continue to search for strategies to cope with the problems of constricting or static budgets and rising costs of materials and personnel coupled with an increasingly demanding and sophisticated user population. In this climate, librarians face mounting pressure to justify acquisitions decisions and differences in the cost and effectiveness of acquisitions methods have assumed increasing importance.

Costs for library materials have risen more steeply than the cost of other goods and services. It is true that rising materials prices have reflected an increase in the cost of production and distribution; the costs of labor, paper, postage and printing have increased dramatically over the past ten years. It is also true, however, that factors peculiar to the nature of scholarship and scholarly publishing have accounted for higher materials prices as well. Although libraries appear to have little impact on the pricing of materials, a critical examination of acquisitions methods and collection development activities may yield a range of strategies to deal with budget and resource stringencies.

The conference papers examine the nature of materials costs and pricing and evaluate methods of materials acquisition. In "Pricing from Three Perspectives: The Publisher, the Wholesaler, the Library," Kent Hendrickson, Dean of Libraries, University of Nebraska, provides a brief history of pricing policies and procedures, with emphasis on the most recent fifteen years. Then, Hendrickson switches the focus to the 1980s and to those factors that are currently impacting pricing, including the economy and automation. Jennifer Cargill, Associate Director of Libraries, Technical Processing, Texas Tech University, examines the cost-effectiveness of approval plan purchasing as opposed to firm orders and other types of acquisitions methods in her paper "The Approval Connection: Pricing the Ordering Alternatives."

Leonard Schrift, President of Ballen Booksellers International, Inc., presents a vendor's perspective in his paper "Truth in Vending." In "Books Across the Waters: An Examination of United Kingdom Mono-

© 1987 by The Haworth Press, Inc. All rights reserved.

graphic Pricing," Dana Alessi, Division Sales Manager, Blackwell North America, discusses how the foreign book trade and pricing differ from the U.S. book trade and pricing. Alessi analyzes the factors which influence the pricing of foreign monographs distributed in the United States to determine why some titles cost less in the United States than the original foreign edition, why others cost the same, and why others more.

George Bauer, Director, University of Oklahoma Press, offers a publisher's viewpoint in "Mountains and Molehills: How University Presses Determine Book Prices and How Those Prices Relate to Library Budgets." Bauer explains how a publisher can quickly determine, by inserting his own house's figures into a simple formula, the price at which he can recover costs on a given book if expectations regarding sales are realized. Examples are given of how the formula works and other factors that influence book prices are explored. In "Acquisition Costs: How the Selection of a Purchasing Source Affects the Cost of Processing Materials," Edna Laughrey, Head, Acquisitions Department, University of Michigan, shows how the dollar value of materials added to library collections should be thought of in broader terms than simply the amount paid for the materials. The four S's, Laughrey maintains, must also be considered: staff, space, supplies and systems.

In "Differential Pricing of Monographs and Serials," Christian Boissonnas, Acquisitions Librarian, Cornell University, examines both the domestic practice of pricing publications differently for individuals and libraries and the English practice of charging prices on the U.S. market which are substantially different from those on the English market. Kit Kennedy, Assistant Director, Academic Information Services, Faxon Company, presents a vendor's viewpoint in her paper, "The Cost of Global Serials: The Vendor's Perspective." Kennedy provides a brief historical perspective on pricing and explores the factors which determine serials costs. She focuses on the productive triangle of library-vendor-publisher within this pricing context.

James T. Stephens, President, EBSCO Industries, Inc., in "The Library's Cost and the Vendor's Price for Serials," reviews serials publisher pricing and serials subscription agency pricing internationally. Library cost factors other than disbursements to vendors are considered for serials. In "Materials Costs and Collection Development in Academic Libraries," Lenore Clark, Coordinator of Collection Development, University of Oklahoma, examines the effect of rising and fluctuating prices on collection management and describes how collection development activities reflect a shift toward positive planned responses to the uncertainties of pricing.

Each of the formal papers presented at the conference was followed by a period of questions to the speaker and discussion among the participants. Unfortunately, the lively and often provocative dialogue cannot be reported here. We are pleased to present the edited conference papers in this volume and hope that the views and insights provided will be meaningful to the reader.

Two other persons contributed to the preparation of this volume. Rodney Hersberger, Director, California State College Library, Bakersfield, provided superb editorial assistance. Pat Webb provided excellent overall administrative support to the Conference and to this book's preparation.

Sul H. Lee
Norman, Oklahoma

Pricing From Three Perspectives: The Publisher, the Wholesaler, the Library

Kent Hendrickson

While taking a few days to decide whether or not to accept this assignment I perused the current literature on the broad subject of publisher/library relations and was surprised to find that there is considerable current interest in pricing. In fact, in 1984 the American Library Association passed a "Resolution Concerning Discounts Received by Public Libraries from Trade Publishers."[1] The resolution protested the higher discounts offered retail bookstores by many trade publishers. It is unlikely this action has had any impact on the discounts received by libraries, but it does reflect an increased concern by librarians. At any rate, I was convinced the topic merits discussion.

The next question probably is, am I qualified to address the topic? I am currently serving as director of a large research library and my opinions will, no doubt, reflect that role. Over the past twenty years, though, I have had a number of experiences and responsibilities with publishers, wholesalers, and libraries that, I believe, provide me with a balanced perspective. Part of my early tenure in academic libraries was spent in an acquisitions department responsible for acquiring both monographs and serials. I was also involved in the negotiations for one of the earliest approval plans. In 1970, for a period of almost a dozen years, I abandoned academe, working for the Richard Abel Company and Blackwell North America. This private sector experience provided the opportunity to learn more about pricing and discounts than anyone would ever want to know. I will mention only three examples: Abel's proposed cost plus pricing scheme; B/NA's attempts at establishing publisher relations following the demise of the Abel company; and the almost monthly manipulating of the B/NA firm order and approval pricing matrices before the firm showed a consistent profit. Last, as further evidence of my credentials, I am an avid consumer of publisher products.

Certainly, the majority of my comments will be directed toward sales to academic libraries because that is where my experience lies. Then too, I will tend to place more emphasis on monographic purchases than journals. However, most of my remarks can be applied to all types of libraries and both material types.

Libraries are entering another critical period in their history. The "Information Age" has brought a heightened awareness of libraries. Many academic libraries in particular are vulnerable because of tightened budgets coupled with rapidly increasing costs and demands for new and improved services. Enrollments have declined at some universities, monetary support from the federal level has decreased, and in a number of states, particularly those located in the farm and energy belts, the dismal state of the economy has forced university-wide retrenchment. In my own state the university system was required to cut its budget by 2 percent at mid-year. This was difficult but in reality we were fortunate when compared to neighboring states.

When university cuts are necessary the library system often is asked to contribute more than its fair share. Other campus costs, including tenured faculty salaries and facilities, are normally fixed and cannot be reduced substantially in the short term. The library faces a similar in-house problem and ends up slicing the materials budget — often the easiest allocation to cut.

In a recent article Jay Lucker describes rather succinctly the many pressures placed on today's academic libraries.

> In attempting to explain why it has been difficult for libraries to increase or even maintain a level of acquisitions that would provide publishers with a less pessimistic view of the present and future, one must also consider some of the peculiarities and limitations of library budgets: (1) the substantial portion allocated to personnel; (2) the compartmentalized nature of library operations; (3) the high cost of making changes and the slow rate at which these changes can be accomplished; (4) the fact that the principal source of income is almost always the institutional appropriation (other sources, such as endowment, gifts, grants, income from fees, charges, and services, represent a much smaller percentage of income); (5) the extremely high fixed costs of maintaining a large storehouse of information; (6) the large expense of maintaining aging collections; (7) the fact that the introduction of new technology seldom reduces operating costs; (8) the proportionally increased cost of providing service as collections grow; (9) the fact that those who benefit from the services and collections are seldom in a decision-making position concerning the budget; and (10) the difficulty of demonstrating the value of a library except when services or collections are reduced.[2]

This would seem to be the appropriate time to interject a word about resource sharing. Personally, I wish we could drop this issue. Most publishers do not seem to have bothered to read the report prepared by King Research, Inc., for the U.S. Copyright Office entitled, *Libraries, Publishers, and Photocopying*.[3] The report should have laid to rest many of their arguments, but based on my discussions with publishers over the past several years it has had little influence.

Publishers should note that more than 99 percent of all research library lending is intracampus.[4] Even when formal efforts are made to increase resource sharing among campuses the results have been less than spectacular. How many of us regularly make a "no buy" decision on the basis of the availability of a needed title in another library? More than likely the decision is still made for either of two reasons: (1) to speed up access or, (2) the item is out-of-print. I am also convinced that most scholars use ILL only as a last resort, if at all, preferring to utilize the resources at hand rather than going through the inconvenience of borrowing elsewhere. No, the problem is not increased resource sharing, it is prices and the demand for new library services.

Picking up where Lucker left off, the impact inflation had on libraries during the 1970s and early 1980s was devastating. Librarians are all painfully aware the cost of books and journals consistently increased at a faster rate than the Consumer Price Index. Since 1970 the average book price has increased by a cumulative 156 percent from $11.66[5] to $30.00;[6] a comparable figure for periodicals reveals a staggering 428 percent increase from $10.41[7] to $54.97.[8]

To illustrate the impact the rate of inflation has had on just one library, let me cite the situation at the University of Nebraska-Lincoln. Although the periodicals budget at the University increased by 410 percent during the period from 1970 to 1985, the end result was the ability to buy approximately the same number of periodical subscriptions as in 1970. Then when one looks at the imbalance the skyrocketing cost of periodicals has created in the materials budget, you begin to feel some sympathy for the book publishers. In 1970 Nebraska spent 30.5 percent of its allocation on periodicals and serials, today it spends 59.5 percent. We purchased 49,600 books in 1970; in 1985 we bought 28,560.

Nebraska is not necessarily the typical academic library. After all the recent Association of Research Libraries annual figures indicate that no less than 13 research libraries spent more than four million dollars each on library materials in fiscal 1984; another 17 spent in excess of three million. A random selection of 25 ARL institutions indicates their combined materials budgets have increased by an average rate of 9.2 percent for the five years up to and including 1984. Not an astronomical increase, but it is ahead of book prices for the same period. In fact, book prices have actually plateaued over the past three years. Are there brighter days ahead? Sorry, I am afraid not. A quote from the August issue of *Library Journal* states:

> The trend of decreasing inflation in periodicals prices of the past two years continued this year. Subscription prices for U.S. periodi-

cals, based on a sample of 3,731 titles, show an average increase of 8.6 percent over 1984 prices, with an average subscription price of $59.70; last year's average subscription price was $54.97, which was an increase of 9.4 percent over 1983. This year's percentage increase is the lowest percentage increase for any year in the current index base year of 1977).[9]

This is the lowest percentage increase in a decade but still well above the current rate of inflation. For most academic libraries the problem is compounded by the faster rate of price increases from British publishers. One distributor of North American and British journals told me their in-house projection for increased journal prices for fiscal 1986 is 19.5 percent. Obviously, any budget increase for many libraries will have to be used to cover current subscriptions. Left-over dollars will probably be needed for new services—not new books or journals.

One of those new services (quickly becoming part of the routine) is on-line searching. On many campuses those librarians servicing the physical and life sciences tell me that on-line searching now requires more of their time than any other aspect of their jobs. Where does the budget support come from? Probably the materials budget. At least in my opinion that is where it should come from; if not we are short changing the scientists because the only alternative is fee-based service. Most of us have at least been partially successful in avoiding that option. To give in to fee based services would accelerate the rush towards being "frozen out" of the information exchange business. Another area finally receiving needed attention is preservation. Up until a few years ago, a relatively small percentage of the materials budget was allocated to binding. Now that library administrators are aware of the critical nature of the preservation issue, binding funds are on the increase, and a few libraries have actually developed special treatment centers within their facilities. Chances are the dollars to support these efforts are once again taken from the materials budget.

Have we reached the time when the library budget will never keep pace with the cost of materials again, or the cost of materials plus new services? Probably so, at least for the foreseeable future. The 1960s was the decade of higher education, both libraries and publishers took advantage of this boom period and played it for all it was worth. Unfortunately the 1960s was followed by the 1970s—the austere 1970s—and the trend continues well into the 1980s. Libraries have less money to spend on an increasing number of books, journals, and other media. Publishers respond by raising prices. When will the spiral end? The recent leveling of book prices, provides only a brief hiatus, but it really does not matter because the price of journals continues to boom along, devouring a disproportionate share of the materials budget.

Not surprisingly librarians are worried about pricing as well as publishers and jobbers who are also concerned about a shrinking library market. It is estimated that all types of libraries in the United States currently spend in excess of 2.5 billion dollars annually on materials. This is one market most publishers cannot afford to ignore, although it is of more importance to the scholarly publishers—scientific and technical, and university. For scholarly publishers the majority of their business is with academic libraries. For the producers of scholarly journals, often their only outlet is these same institutions along with special libraries. The concern is real on all sides, more so than anytime in the history of publisher/wholesaler/library relations.

Although a well documented history of library/book trade relations in North America does not exist, it is clear that the two most frequently mentioned causes of discord between the two groups are the issues of copyright and pricing. The former receives the most press, but the latter is the more enduring irritant.

When the 1876 American Library Association Conference took place in Philadelphia, the first attempt by the book trade to fix the retail price of books was being made, and only a 20 percent discount from list was allowed to libraries. In response the conference passed the following resolution:

> Resolved, that the discrimination against libraries in the rules of the American Bookseller's Association, which forbids the trade from supplying libraries with books at a greater discount than twenty percent, is unjust and impolitic and is a rule which no librarian is bound to respect.[10]

A committee was formed to deal with the publishers, but by early the next year *Publishers' Weekly* reported: "Reform has become a mockery, the American Book Trade Association almost a myth, the twenty percent rule a thirty percent rule."[11]

In May 1901, the American Publishers' Association and the American Booksellers' Association drafted an agreement which though unsuccessful was to set a pattern for bookselling up to the present day. The agreement was initially applauded by librarians as a positive reform. They were supportive because their suppliers—local bookstores—were being forced out of business by the predecessors of the Crowns and Barnes and Nobles of today, the dry goods and department stores. They had begun to sell books as an advertisement at a very low profit, so the bookstores could not compete. Under the new rules, for those books that were published at "net," exclusive of juveniles and school books, retailers agreed not to discount the titles for a period of one year, after which they were free to give any discount they chose. There were exceptions to the no discount rule, the libraries being one, as they were granted a discount of 10 percent.[12]

Although the discount afforded libraries for that first controlled year was generally increased over the next few years, their initial support for the agreement quickly turned sour. Since libraries were able to negotiate for discounts in excess of the new limit under the previous open bargaining arrangement, publishers initially stated they would reduce the list price of books so that the net price would be fair compensation for the loss in discount. For example, a book once priced at $1.50 and formerly sold to the average library for $1.00 would now be listed at $1.25 minus 10 percent. Granted, this was still a sizeable increase for libraries but a price they were willing to pay as long as they were provided ready access to more titles through local retailers. Not surprisingly, prices did not come down. Publishers claimed that increased costs, binding and illustrations in particular, made it impossible for them to reduce their prices.[13]

By 1907 the Publisher's Association gave up its attempts at "price fixing," influenced by a number of judicial decisions that led it to believe the agreement with booksellers was probably in "restraint of trade." After 1907, all agreements were to be made between individual publishers and the dealers they supplied.[14]

The American Publishers' Association (and its successors) continued efforts at what came to be called "price maintenance" well into the 20th century. They were most successful during the 1930s and 1940s, first through the short-lived National Recovery Act, and later through enactment by several states of fair trade laws. These laws generally dictated that the retailer could not resell below the agreed to "fair trade price" for a stated period, usually six months to one year. The publishers' supporting argument was libraries are competition; the librarians' rebuttal was we serve the public good and promote book sales.[15]

Gradually the ineffectiveness of the fair trade laws led to their demise. Today the Robinson-Patnam Act of 1936 provides the legal guidance for publishers. Trade publishers (in fact all types of publishers) must generally offer a range of discounts that are dependent on the quantity of the order. Robinson-Patnam states that the discount can vary only when doing so reflects a real cost savings for the manufacturer, for example trade publishers routinely offer bookstores higher discounts if they agree to provide promotional advertising for individual titles. That is the law we live by and it is the interpretation of that law that was brought into question by the aforementioned 1984 ALA resolution.

Perhaps it is finally time to bring the book and journal wholesalers — jobbers, vendors, etc. — on stage. Their growth has been one of the more interesting developments in the book distribution business in this country. Their position is unique since in most businesses the wholesaler is the middleman, between the producer and the retailer. Most often they serve consumers not served by the retailers. In the book business, wholesalers may serve both retail outlets and libraries. How this particular phenomenon developed is described by John P. Dessauer:

> Prior to the War and the Depression, many book sellers served their local public and educational libraries, thus enlarging their income and increasing their value to their communities. When the wholesalers absorbed this function, they in fact competed with these retailers and, we might add, in a most remarkable way. They persuaded the publishers to continue to extend, or even to increase, the discount they had received when they were still purchasing books for resale to retailers, and in turn offered to libraries (on a contract basis) an up-to-then unprecedented discount roughly equivalent to that which they might have given to the retailers they were abandoning.[16]

The result was the development of a lucrative market for wholesalers—libraries—and the weakening of the retail outlets. Wholesalers have continued to expand their library advantage, particularly since the 1940s by offering additional services, including cataloging, processing, approval plans, and more generous return privileges. These are services that publishers and retail stores are either unwilling or unable to provide. Hence, even if the discount from the wholesaler is marginally less than from the publisher, the extra services plus the ability to deal with one or two suppliers rather than several hundred is seen as a real advantage. In effect, everyone benefits, publishers aren't bothered with piles of small orders; libraries keep their paperwork to a minimum; and wholesalers have a greater spread between their buying and selling price than in the retail market. Only the poor retailer is left on the outside looking in.

If there is one characteristic common to all aspects of the bookselling business it is the low profit margin. Very few individuals get rich in this business, and those that do were probably bought out by CBS. One recent writer commenting on trade publishing noted that, "On the average, three in ten titles are marginally profitable, 30% break even, and the remainder lose money."[17] Most scholarly commercial publishers face even tighter pressures. Libraries are perhaps fortunate that university presses are nonprofit organizations, although many are under increased pressures to at least break even. The cost of paper (the major cost for publishers) increased by 70 percent during the 70s, and in one year alone the cost of binding, printing and labor increased by 20 percent[18]—evidence that libraries were not alone in their losing battle with inflation.

Add to all these factors the 1979 Thor Power Tool Decision which among other things stopped publishers from any longer writing down inventories for tax purposes. "Thor" has had a triple impact: (1) Shorter print runs, which means a title goes out of print faster; (2) The cost of manufacturing is spread over fewer books; and, (3) Most publishers now raise the price of backlisted titles along with current titles. To cite just one example of the impact both inflation and "Thor" have had on university presses, the University of Nebraska Press' print runs averaged between 1,500 and 2,000 copies during most of the 1970s, 1200 to 1500 by 1980, and are down to 900 to 1200 copies today.

The same inflationary trends have contributed to the rising prices of journals. Publishers of journals also blame resource sharing, and the pressure from publish or perish that has resulted in many new journals with limited markets. The latter two arguments are made to support the contention that fewer subscriptions result in the costs being spread over fewer copies. This may be the case, but publishers also realize that the periodicals allocation is the least elastic of all library budgets. We simply will not cancel a title when we already have the first 90 volumes on the shelf. Who wants their shelves filled with incomplete sets? Finally, let me share a piece of incriminating evidence concerning libraries shared by a publisher of scientific journals. His firm performed a market survey after experiencing several years of declining market share. It determined that when forced to cancel one of two journals covering the same general subject matter, academic libraries will cancel the least expensive title. The firm's conclusion was to raise prices to the same level or above those of its competition.

Although several of my former colleagues might argue with me, I feel many book wholesalers benefited from the high inflation of the late 1970s, early 1980s. The successful wholesaler was able to offer libraries higher discounts than previously and still reap larger profits. The reason being that their operating costs did not keep pace with the price of books. (If book prices continue to hold at their current levels, these discounts will begin to slip.) Nonetheless, wholesalers also work on a very small margin, ranging somewhere between 23 percent and 32 percent depending on the size of the operation and the types of libraries being supplied. Compare this to the 40 percent realized by the largest discount stores, and 100 percent and more by many retail outlets. Wholesalers also face a shrinking market since libraries are not buying more books. This has undoubtedly influenced Baker and Taylor's aggressive move back into the retail bookstore arena.

A top executive with one of the major wholesalers informed me that for the current fiscal year his company's budget is based on an inflationary rate of 2.5 percent, down from 14 percent just two years previously. Discounts to academic libraries average 6 to 7 percent compared to 2 to 3 percent three years ago, and approvals are going out at 10 to 11 percent compared to the previous 7 to 8.

Having talked with representatives from several wholesalers, it is obvious that automation is more of a factor for the largest firms. Several are able to pass OCLC, RLG, and WLN generated orders directly into their own computer systems. Those that can, realize a substantial savings in processing costs and do not pass on the out of pocket costs to the customer. Obviously, automation will play an even larger role for all book suppliers in the near future. Currently, one large wholesaler is receiving 8 percent of all domestic orders electronically, up from 2 percent just one year ago.

Automation can also influence the negotiations carried on between wholesalers and libraries. Traditionally, wholesalers have indicated that both volume and mix of order types influenced any flat discount they might offer an individual library. However, only in recent years have they been able to measure these factors, particularly order mix. Automation has made this possible and several wholesalers now regularly make the flat discount option available to firm order customers.

How can libraries influence pricing? One scientific/technical publisher's response to that question was a simple "they can't." He knows what he has to make on each book he publishes and if the library is willing to pay the price, fine, if not, that's fine too, and he lives with the decision. As an aside, he told me that authors of scholarly monographs often have a large influence on the ultimate price. They do this not as a favor to libraries but as a favor to their colleagues. If they can convince the publisher a lower price will sell more books, the publisher will often go along. Alternatively, for obvious reasons, authors of journal articles have no such influence. Did you also know that a fairly common practice among commercial publishers of scholarly works is to require the author to commit to the purchase of 200 to 300 copies of his or her own printed publication? Could this be a possible contribution to the leveling of book prices?

My comments on the ways to influence pricing will actually be quite brief. Contrary to the remark by the scientific/technical publisher, I am impressed by the influence librarians are currently having, most likely more than at any other time in the history of library/book trade relations. Namely, the development of two journals, *Library Acquisitions: Practice and Theory* and *Serials Librarian*, has provided a forum for discussion of the very topics addressed in this volume. You might say that librarians now have a counter to *Publishers' Weekly*. A scan through *Library Literature* or a computer search brings to one's attention numerous articles on pricing, discounts, jobber relations, etc. A publisher of scientific journals told me that comments within the library literature influenced his company to reduce the price differential between what is being offered individual subscribers and libraries. Several British journal publishers have agreed to hold prices at current levels for several years partially as a reaction to American librarians' charges of price gouging.

The overriding barrier that acquisitions librarians must face when dealing with booksellers is to recognize and accept the fact that they are negotiating with a commercial business. To the sales representative the "bottom line" is the primary pricing consideration. There are still many acquisitions librarians who are intimidated by the thought of having to haggle over price. I have met several recently who admit to leaving price entirely out of their purchasing decisions, focusing instead on other service aspects.

A dear friend, James Cameron, who spent many years selling to academic libraries, used to say that for the majority of libraries the decision on where to buy is based on who they know and like best personally or on who visited the library last. There are others who simply spread the business around, preferring not to offend any of the sales representatives. The rationale often given for the latter approach is the avoidance of "all the eggs in one basket." The Richard Abel demise occurred more than ten years ago but it is continuing to have its influence, and those librarians who are writing current policy based on that unfortunate bit of history are not making solid business decisions. It may be that by placing more orders with a single vendor a library can make that shrinking dollar carry further.

Before one can "deal" he or she must have a reasonably good understanding of the total book trade. Take the time to visit with a local press, learn about their problems. I encourage you to read *In Cold Type: Overcoming the Book Crises* by Leonard Shatzkin.[19] This is a fascinating book about the trade, not just because it taught me a few new things, but because it has an excellent section on the economics of publishing, and on the steps the industry must take if it is to survive.

One of the more interesting developments in the wholesaler/library relationship area is the relatively recent changes that have occurred in the bid system. Fortunately, these changes are progressive, bringing us a long way from the New York state type systems of the late 1970s. Such systems offered unrealistically high bids by suppliers, with resulting unacceptable fulfillment rates for libraries, and no state agency to monitor performance. There was also the additional prospect for libraries of having to switch suppliers annually. In those states where the bid system existed, it has either been dropped completely or replaced by an approved vendor list. In Ohio, wholesalers submit prices for various categories of books. The prices are published along with the terms of sale. Libraries buying under these terms can assume that both the services and discounts will remain in effect for two years. No library is required to use the approved wholesalers but in most instances it is to their advantage to do so.[20]

The most successful of all the approved vendor list approaches appears to be operating in North Carolina, so successful that it is a bit surprising more states have not adopted it. Each year acquisitions librarians representing some 40 institutions of higher education meet with wholesaler representatives to discuss service and discounts. From the group of wholesalers who choose to attend the meeting, two are selected for the approved list. Each agrees to provide a specified discount for all firm orders for a one year period. The wholesalers are evaluated on the basis of service provided and at the end of 12 months a new round of negotiations takes place. The attraction for vendors is a potentially large market for firm orders. For the individual library there are several benefits: (1) guaranteed discounts; (2) interaction with other libraries in the vendor review process; (3) increased contact with vendors; and (4) since the contract is not binding, the library is free to deal with other wholesalers if service is not acceptable from either of the vendors on the list.[21]

My discussions with several librarians familiar with the North Carolina system indicate that the system continues to be a success after ten years of operation. I recommended more librarians consider this approach.

Other libraries and consortia may have other methods for influencing prices and discounts. What is clear, is that more pressure is being placed on both wholesaler and publisher to provide fair and equitable prices. I am reminded of a time in late 1980, prior to leaving B/NA, when I was asked to participate in a meeting at OCLC along with representatives from other wholesalers. The topic of that meeting was the proposed OCLC pass through system for the handling of firm orders. This is the same system many libraries and wholesalers are now using. The main concern expressed by all the wholesalers present was that libraries not be given the capability to compare discounts offered on specific titles by jobbers. We did not wish to see management reports flowing from the system. In retrospect that all seems rather short-sighted and naive. Such comparisons were and are inevitable having been made easier through automation. Libraries should utilize every tool available to them and I encourage them to do so.

What about the future? The issues described in this paper are not likely to disappear. I am not one of those who predict that in five or ten years we may look back on the 80s as the good years, but the 1960s and early 1970s certainly weren't part of the normal cycle. Those exceptional years for libraries are gone forever.

An area that will have an increasing impact on publishing and libraries is electronic publishing. How much of an impact, no one knows. Will libraries be able to replace their hard-copy subscriptions to scientific journals with the electronic, on-line variety? Not likely, existing journal and book collections will need to be maintained and developed for many years. There is even evidence that some publishers are beginning to question the wisdom of plunging headlong into electronic publishing. Originally they viewed the electronic format as a supplement to, not a replacement for, the hard-copy and they are concerned that the latter may actually be occurring. All that librarians can be sure of is that prices will inevitably continue to rise no matter what the format.

The challenge is still there for librarians: stretching limited resources to meet needs, responding to present demands from our users for information in traditional print formats, while actively participating in the new information handling process.

NOTES

1. Eaglen, Audrey B., "Publishers' Trade Discounts: A Simple Matter of Fairness," *School Library Journal*, 30 (May 1984):29.
2. Lucker, Jay K., "Publishers and Librarians: Reflections of a Research Library Administrator," *Library Quarterly*, 54 (January 1984):57.
3. McDonald, Dennis D., and Bush, Colleen G., with King, Donald W., et al., *Libraries, Publishers, and Photocopying: Final Report of Surveys Conducted for the United States Copyright Office*. Rockville, MD: King Research Co., 1982.
4. Rothstein, Samuel, "The Extended Library and the Dedicated Library: A Sceptical Outsider Looks at Union Catalogues and Bibliographic Networks," The Future of the Union Catalogue: Proceedings of the International Symposium on the Future of the Union Catalogue," *Cataloging and Classification Quarterly*, 2 (1982):110.
5. Atkinson, Hugh C., "Prices of U.S. and Foreign Published Materials" in *Bowker Annual of Library and Book Trade Information 1972*. New York, R.R. Bowker, 1972, p. 185.
6. Grannis, Chandler B., "Title Output and Average Prices: 1984 Final Figures," *Publishers' Weekly*, 228 (August 23, 1985):43
7. Atkinson, p. 183.
8. Horn, Judith G. and Lenzini, Rebecca T., "Price Indexes for 1985: U.S. Periodicals," *Library Journal*, 110 (August 1985):57.
9. *Ibid.*, p. 55.
10. Orman, Oscar C., *Library Discount Control: A Survey to January 1940; With a Supplementary Report to January 1941*. Chicago, American Library Association, 1941, p. 1.
11. "Reduction of Retail Prices," *Publishers' Weekly*, 11 (February 10, 1877):163.
12. Lord, Isabel Ely, "Some Notes on the Principles and Practice of Bookbuying for Libraries," *Library Journal*, 32 (January, 1907):3–11.
13. *Ibid.*
14. "Plan of the American Publishers' Association Adopted at a Meeting Held January 9, 1907," *Library Journal*, 32 (January 1907):20.
15. Orman, pp. 13–49 passim.
16. Dessauer, John P., "Introducing 'The Funnel'—A Regional Processing Center to Handle All Book Transactions," *Publishers' Weekly*, 202 (November 27, 1972):24.
17. Compaine, Benjamin M., *The Book Industry in Transition: An Economic Study of Book Distribution and Marketing*. White Plains, NY: Knowledge Industry Publications, Inc., 1978. p. 20.
18. *Ibid.*, pp. 20–21.
19. Shatzkin, Leonard, *In Cold Type: Overcoming the Book Crises*. Boston, Houghton Mifflin Co., 1972.
20. Alley, Brian, "Library Bids, Contracts, and Price Agreements," Presented at the Midwinter Meeting of the American Library Association, 1981, Bethesda, MD, ERIC Document Reproduction Service, ED 201 311, 1981.
21. Lindsey, Jonathan A., "Vendor Discounts to Libraries in a Consortium," *Library Acquisitions: Practice and Theory*, 5 (1981):147–152.

The Approval Connection: Pricing the Ordering Alternatives

Jennifer Cargill

Libraries are increasingly pressed to meet the needs of their different levels of clientele; they are facing budgetary restraints at the same time that buying needs are increasing and becoming more diverse. Since Richard Abel and his successors in other companies devised the Approval Plan as we know it today, Approval Programs have become an acceptable means of acquiring a large portion of materials the academic library purchases. While we are familiar with the use of approval programs as collection development and acquisitions tools, what about approval programs and other ordering alternatives from the viewpoint of cost to the organization? Are these ordering methods cost effective mechanisms? Where are the cost savings?

First, what are our primary responsibilities as librarians? What are we trying to accomplish in meeting the goals of our institutions in our positions as *managers of resources, developers of collections, distributors of services,* and *conveyors of knowledge?*

The 1980s have been termed by some as the period of the new three "Rs" in higher education—"Reduction, Reallocation, and Retrenchment"—or "Cut, Squeeze, and Trim" administration.[1] As the *managers of resources*, we must be concerned with expending these resources efficiently yet effectively. These resources are possibly limited in size, and are probably governed by internal and/or external regulations. They may also be public funds and subject to fluctuation as the state's economy changes. We are in the position of wanting to meet the goals of our own organization, using available resources to meet organizational objectives, but also wanting to minimize salary and other costs associated with the process of acquiring the materials and providing access to them. If we are dealing with declining or zero growth resources, this is especially critical. If we are faced with the pleasant situation of increasing funding, we will want to satisfy institutional needs without committing too large a portion of our resources to personnel costs which we may find we are unable to support later. At the same time, we want to expend funds quickly and speed the materials into the library collection, making them accessible to our demanding patrons.

As the *developers of collections,* we want to acquire the materials needed by our clientele for meeting institutional curricular needs, fulfilling scholars' research demands—to the extent it is reasonable and possible—narrowing gaps in collecting patterns, stimulating users' interests in the collection, and, when appropriate, acquiring some special unique items. Today, of course, the term "collections" encompasses many formats and may require the acquisition of special equipment to provide access to some of the formats in the collection.

In our role as *distributors of services*, we utilize these resources—both monetary and personnel—to provide effective, nonfrustrating access to the collection. This may take the form of increased user instruction, augmented computer search services, or online access to the collections's database.

Finally, as *conveyors of knowledge*, we cannot husband resources so closely that we control or eliminate access to the detriment of our clientele. We state in the "Library Bill of Rights": ". . . that all libraries are forums of information and ideas . . ."[2] and in our professional interpretation of this document, we state: "We will make available to everyone who needs or desires them the widest possible diversity of views and modes of expression, including those which are strange, unorthodox or unpopular."[3]

How do we use acquisitions alternatives to accomplish these goals? Are the approval plans and other ordering mechanisms cost effective ways to satisfy these goals? We must look at three groups of factors in considering costs:

1. The external factors:
2. The collection development factor; and
3. The internal acquisitions and processing factors.

EXTERNAL FACTORS

As *conveyors of knowledge* and *developers of collections*, we are committed to acquiring materials as quickly as possible. As resource managers, we also want our methods to be as cost effective as possible. *External factors* certainly affect our ability to reach this objective. In order to do so, we must be knowledgeable of the publishing and vending world ourselves or have the foresight to employ personnel with this expertise. Such personnel should be aware of the institutional goals so they can be relied upon to seek the best financial savings for the library and provide the best service. Whether we are the administrators hiring such personnel or the person being hired for such a position, we must be aware of the best ways to acquire materials speedily. Acquiring materials with dispatch can also mean significant cost savings both in the acquisitions and processing procedures.

When a library commits a portion of its materials budget to an approval program, several *external factors* enter the picture. As discussed in Frye and Romanansky's paper[4] from the 1983 University of Oklahoma conference, there are four phases or cycles of the product marketing program for a book. As the authors of that paper cautioned, no two books will have exactly the same product life cycle. In the first phase of the product life cycle, the Market Introduction Phase, when the book is being initially presented to its potential users, most of them are unaware that it even exists. Most acquirers of the book in this stage—for our purposes the first library to own the book—obtain it through an approval program or on standing order. Today with short print runs for so many books, these initial purchasers will utilize a large portion, perhaps even a majority, of the copies printed.

Those libraries without automatic acquisitions programs may begin to obtain the book at the next marketing phase that is identified by Frye and Romanansky: the Market Growth Phase. It is during this stage that advertisements appear in the media, flyers are mailed, and the book is reviewed.

During the last two stages—the Market Maturity Phase and the Sales Decline Phase—the book may become more difficult to obtain. As Frye and Romanansky state: "The approval plan provides the book with exposure to its marketplace earlier in the cycle. Sales for the title will therefore peak earlier."[5]

Obviously, if a library can acquire the book in the initial phase, it will have taken advantage of the entire marketing process and the materials will be in house or en route before demand has peaked—or perhaps even before it becomes of interest. If the library delays until phase two or three or four, there is a greater possibility of not acquiring the book at all.

A few years ago, prior to the Thor ruling, when a print run was almost exhausted, if the book was selling, the publisher might reprint. Now if a publisher does reprint a book in demand, reprinting costs may be higher if labor, paper, or other costs have increased. Today there is a good chance the book will go out-of-print quickly. Unfortunately, reporting of current year imprints as being out-of-print is no longer a phenomenon. Acquiring books on the out-of-print market can be both elusive and expensive.

With foreign publications, there is in addition to the possibility of short runs or limited printings, slowness in securing bibliographic data and, therefore, in even identifying the existence of the material. As we know, with purchasing of foreign library materials, there is sometimes a problem of unusual business practices in a few areas of the world, or of unstable political situations that complicate acquiring materials. A foreign approval plan, or blanket order plan, will ease this acquisitions process simply by helping insure the identification and acquisition of needed material. The process of identifying the existence of a foreign item that fits the library's collection needs may be more complex because foreign bibliographies may not be comprehensive, listing of new publications may not be as readily available, and responses to inquiries to publishers may be nonexistent. With foreign approval or blanket plans, one *external factor* is particularly important: "...the vendor on the spot can select the books and send them directly to the library. Chances are that in most cases the books are in the library long before the scholar comes looking for specific titles after reading reviews of them."[6]

These *external factors* introduce cost elements that are admittedly difficult to quantify in actual dollars and cents because they entail:

- Identifying materials the library did not acquire because the material was unknown to the library staff. It is virtually impossible to determine how much this lack of identification will cost library collections.
- Establishing what was not acquired because of short print runs, limited printings, unusual business practices or unstable political conditions is similarly difficult to quantify but costly to the library.
- Determining what the cost was to the collection because the library attempted to acquire items too late in their product life cycle may be identifiable when purchase is made on the out-of-print market (a costly process) or in a later reprinting when the cost has increased substantially.

Acquisition of ongoing series via standing order or of books on approval programs introduces automatic purchasing methods that are to some extent immune to many of these *external factors*. If we can get materials into our collections with minimal interference from market strategies, publishing problems, or business and political issues, we can then concentrate our collecting efforts elsewhere.

In assessing the cost to the collection of these external factors, we may find that the true costs may not be discovered until years later.

COLLECTION DEVELOPMENT FACTORS

Moving from those *external factors* that have a cost impact, let us consider the *collection development factors* and their bearing on costs of materials.

A part of our responsibility for being collection developers is to insure relevant coverage of subjects needed for the curriculum and research, fill in gaps, and provide comprehensiveness where appropriate. Many libraries do not have collection development policies. Designing approval plan profiles or establishing standing orders forces us to examine our collection needs and identify areas where the curriculum and research interests necessitate purchasing of materials. Often establishment of an approval program will be the first time a library staff has defined the collection scope and this may even lead to writing of formal collection policies.

This examination of profile options also leads to more comprehensive knowledge of our collections, more systematic acquisitions, and spreads coverage through needed subject areas rather than narrowing coverage. An approval program or the establishment of other automatic acquisitions procedures such as standing orders forces us to articulate our collection development objectives, resulting in a better use of our resources to meet the goals of the library.

The existence of an approval profile or a standing order list can also form the skeletal basis of a formal collection development policy. Establishing our collection needs by accepting that "selection begins with the profile"[7] means that a carefully designed profile or standing order list will lead to the meeting of current collection needs through automatic receipt of material. For the selector, this means that numerous advertisements, reviews, and bibliographies need not be relied upon for current material identification. In one study, reported by Emery, it was determined that approval plans resulted in a 10 percent time saving for the selectors.[8] Emery also related his finding that there was a definite time lag if initiation of orders waited for firm order selection.[9]

Librarians today are responsible for many activities. They must be multi-talented, trained in many tasks. Their duties may encompass: collection development, user instruction, and database searching, as well as reference and/or technical processing duties. Added to this may be some administrative responsibilities. Any way that tasks can be accomplished more efficiently—while also being effective—is helpful. In a study of acquisitions methods, respondents reported that transferring their efforts from searching announcements to reviewing receipts enabled them to save from a few minutes to as much as two positions.[10] The collection development responsibilities remain with the selectors but they are judging the new books and freeing large blocks of their time for other responsibilities such as user instruction or for retrospective collection development and assessment. Rather than the selector monitoring hundreds of announcements or catalogs and perusing reviewing sources, the vendor performs those tasks. Rather than keeping track of which publishing firms disappear and to what firm they sell their backlist or identifying new publishing houses as they are created, the vendor does the monitoring.

Of course the selector remains abreast of the literature in the fields for which he or she is responsible, but the pressure of identifying current purchasing needs *before* the print runs vanish is no longer present. Instead, time can be expended on collection assessment, writing formal collection policies, determining new or changing course offerings which may need retrospective purchasing (or rushing current purchasing for new subject offerings), and identifying areas of the collection that suffered from neglect in past years. Many libraries have found that automatic receipt programs will satisfy 75-85 percent of their acquisition needs. This represents a substantial amount of individual, title-by-title identification that is unnecessary. That staff time can be redirected to other tasks, thus eliminating the employment of additional personnel. Harvey and Spyers-Duran reported that library staffing was virtually the same in the 1980s as in the 1970s while publishing volume had continued to increase.[11] It is increasingly important to do more with less, and this situation appears likely to remain with us for the foreseeable future.

Personnel costs are among our largest budget lines. As staff can be freed to concentrate on other tasks, the need for cost savings can be met in other ways. The databases of vendors, particularly approval plan or standing order vendors, can also be used effectively to assist in retrospective purchasing, for examples. Among those ways:

— Identifying titles in a subject area not previously collected by the library by asking the vendor to provide bibliographic data for items published in the specific subject area.
— Identifying titles published during a particular time frame when the library might have had severe budgetary restraints or cutbacks or collection development was not being performed systematically.
— Matching of a vendor's approval tapes against a library's machine readable tapes of its own collection.[12] This matching has not been done that frequently thus far but as more libraries are able to provide tapes, this use of technology may increase. The end product of this tape comparison is identification of titles the library does not own.

When a library uses one vendor primarily, additional interfacing among standing orders, approval plans, and firm order processes will also be possible. All these examples of making technology work for us represent ways to save staff time and redirect energies toward other projects.

Some libraries prefer to receive series via approval. The reasons are good:

— better discounts;
— receive only items in a series that match the profile; and
— receipts can be processed as part of an approval shipment.

Some admonitions if you choose to try receipt of series on approval rather than establishing standing orders:

—For some series for which all numbers should be obtained, if they are received within the approval program, all numbers in the series may not match the profile, resulting in gaps. The discount can be negated by the expense of correcting the situation.
—Selection staff must be made aware that only items matching the profile will be received and they must agree to this concept. This is an education process that must take place to offset the "receive every number" philosophy of collection development.

A matter always of concern to selectors, the acquisitions staff, and the library administrators is the cost of materials. With standing orders, there may be some cost saving through making an ongoing commitment to the publisher or vendor to acquire the materials as published. If one places a large number of standing orders with a single vendor, there may be a minor cost savings—but there may also be a service charge. Receiving numbers of standing orders in large batched shipments may result in some staff and processing savings.

With approval plans, and to some extent standing orders, the vendor purchases in large quantity and therefore may receive a larger discount which in turn may be passed on to the customer, thus providing better discounts. In addition there may be the perquisite of free shipping. With some foreign vendors who offer free shipping, this may result in the equivalent of a 5 percent discount, an important factor since foreign acquisitions may otherwise not carry any discount.

Another cost advantage if a library opts for a flat discount on approval is that this guaranteed discount can be relied upon for a period of time, eliminating concerns with:

—being at the mercy of a fluctuating economy; and
—minimizing a library's concerns about price increases.

In addition, there may be a price consideration just in receiving books early on approval rather than waiting to firm order them. A recent study of more than 300 titles supplied on approval indicated that the prices of 19 percent of the books had increased within a year. By acquiring the books earlier on approval, libraries enjoyed the benefit of the lower cost.

INTERNAL ACQUISITIONS AND PROCESSING FACTORS

We have reviewed external and collection development factors that may affect costs. What about cost factors within internal *acquisitions and processing*? Already mentioned are staff labor and time savings in conjunction with the identification and selection of materials.

Space and personnel needs may actually have priority over material needs. However, it may be easier to get monies for additional materials than for new staff or space.[13] It is easier in tight money periods as well as in affluent periods to use approval plans as an effective way to meet the collection needs with minimal staff attention. Similarly, in the acquisitions department, approval plans are a more efficient acquisition process, utilizing fewer staff to handle shipments. Depending upon internal procedures, from one-fourth to one-third of the staff can process approval receipts as is necessary to process three to four times as many firm orders.

At the 1984 University of Oklahoma conference on "Issues in Acquisitions," Hodge reported the number of classified staff utilized to handle firm orders and approval at one institution. Almost 5000 books were being processed per staff member working on approval receipts as opposed to about 1300 firm order books being processed per staff member.[14] While these figures do not reflect the librarians' time involved in the process, it does represent substantial staff savings in acquiring the materials. Emery reported firm orders as being more than four times as costly as approval items to select, search and verify, and to order and receive.[15]

They also save considerable time and labor in processing invoices for payment, following up on firm orders, and checking status reports. To quote the late Daniel Melcher:

> It's hard enough to get one wholesaler to serve you the way you want to be served, without trying to get 30 to 100 publishers all doing the same thing your way.[16]

While a knowledgeable, on-top-of-the situation acquisitions librarian will insist that a wholesaler meets the library's order fulfillment and invoicing requirements, it is certainly impossible to obtain equally satisfactory performance from individual publishers. With approval shipments, with one invoice and slips with the bibliographic data being supplied, speed of processing and labor cost savings may be significant. One library estimated more than a nine-minute-per-item gross savings for each approval title versus each firm order title. That library estimated that an approval plan of only 6200 titles could result in a savings of seventy-nine hours per month in the technical processing of the receipts.[17]

Once the approval items leave acquisitions further cost savings accrue because 75–90 percent of the titles can be cataloged promptly through the bibliographic utility to which the library belongs. This prompt processing means staff time saved—and therefore a cost savings—as well as putting the books on the shelf more quickly:

— Books are not held for cataloging to become available.
— Repeated researching of the database—now at .06 cents a search on OCLC—becomes unnecessary.

—Costly original cataloging is avoided for items that cannot await availability of online records.

One university library, which insists on anonymity, did a study which showed that firm order books cost three times more to catalog than those received on approval. My own experience supports that conclusion.

There are other cost advantages to approval plans over firm orders, some of which can also be applied to standing orders:

—Management reports and analyses of receipts are available from the approval vendors—as well as from some subscription agencies. These alone can save the time of staff in performing in-house bookkeeping and analyzing of receipts. These reports are particularly helpful in collection development and in analyzing publishing trends.
—Approval books can be returned for full credit and without writing for permission. This is not always true of firm orders.
—Keyboarding, whether on typewriter or computer terminal, is minimized.
—Duplication of work, such as searching and verifying at several points, is decreased.
—The sorting, filing, mailing tasks are reduced or eliminated. Paper shuffling is certainly reduced.
—Routine tasks are shifted to a second party—the vendor—allowing the library to do internal redirecting of staff efforts.
—Discount rate is known in advance, saving time in the vendor selection process.
—Duplication of selection effort is lessened. Studies have shown that of approval books returned to the vendor, most are usually reordered within a few months.

There is also an undiscussed cost benefit: your clout with the vendor. A library with a substantial, well-managed approval program or standing order list has a certain advantage when negotiating discounts or service charges, resolving fulfillment problems, or dealing with other acquisitions matters.

Mention must be made of R. R. Bowker's recently announced decision requiring libraries to obtain Bowker publications on standing order direct from the publisher rather than through jobbers. Bowker is offering a 5 percent discount as an incentive. This discount will quickly be offset by the necessity of generating orders for Bowker standing orders separate from the standing order list placed with jobbers. The discount offered by Bowker will not offset the labor and processing costs. Libraries will also have to endure the start-up period as Bowker establishes a customer fulfillment staff large enough to serve capably the needs of a large volume of library customers.

TECHNOLOGY

There are other reasons for using automatic purchasing programs whether they be approval or standing orders. Technology has developed to the point where we can interface different acquisitions methods, thus eliminating some duplication. Interfacing of different online systems and the loading of tapes with bibliographic data can speed processing. Automatic identification of collection needs frees us for more rewarding, stimulating endeavors. We should *use* developing technology to help us perform our responsibilities and to make us more effective. As mentioned previously, use of technology allows us to compare our own machine readable collection tapes against vendor's databases in order to provide more comprehensive collection analysis. Compare that process to the task of checking traditional published bibliographies against the card catalog!

Automation has made it possible to demystify routine tasks—and speed them up—freeing us for other responsibilities, allowing us to prove our competence in performing these other functions. Automation allows us to use personnel for a wider variety of public and technical tasks. Of course, some people may be resistant to change and initial additional costs may be incurred as we retrain or lose experienced staff or hire new people who must then be trained.

SUMMARY

The result of selecting the best ordering mechanisms and incorporating technology into our libraries will be improved performance in our important role of *distributors of services* and *conveyors of knowledge*. Staff can devote time to quality reference services, train end users, market library services, and solicit additional support for the library which will be recognized for its effective support of institutional goals.

NOTES

1. Kathryn McDonald, "Learning to Finance Learning: A Review Report," *College Board Review* 116 (Summer 1980):129.
2. "Library Bill of Rights," in *Library Acquisitions Policies and Procedures*, 2d ed., edited by Elizabeth Futas, Phoenix: Oryx Press, 1984, p. 557.
3. "Intellectual Freedom Statement: An Interpretation of the Library Bill of Rights," in *Library Acquisitions Policies and Procedures*, 2d ed., edited by Elizabeth Futas. Phoenix: Oryx Press, 1984, pp. 562-564.

4. Gloria Frye and Marcia Romanansky, "The Approval Plan—The Core of an Academic Wholesaler's Business," in *Issues in Acquisitions: Programs and Evaluation*, edited by Sul H. Lee. Ann Arbor, MI: The Pierian Press, 1984, pp. 113-114.
5. Ibid, p. 114.
6. Robert G. Sewell, "Managing European Automatic Acquisitions," *Library Resources and Technical Services* 27 (1983):403.
7. Kathleen McCullough, Edwin D. Posey, and Doyle C. Pickett, *Approval Plans and Academic Libraries*, Phoenix: Oryx Press, p. 139.
8. C. David Emery, "Efficiency and Effectiveness: Approval Plans from a Management Perspective," in *Shaping Library Collections for the 1980s*, edited by Peter Spyers-Duran and Thomas Mann, Jr. Phoenix: Oryx Press, 1980, p. 188.
9. Ibid., p. 199.
10. McCullough, Posey, and Pickett, op. cit., pp. 95-97.
11. John F. Harvey and Peter Spyers-Duran, "The Effect of Inflation on Academic Libraries," *Austerity Management in Academic Libraries*. Metuchen, NJ: Scarecrow, 1984, pp. 1-42.
12. Dana L. Alessi, "Coping with Library Needs: The Approval Vendor's Response/Responsibility," in *Issues in Acquisitions: Program and Evaluation*, edited by Sul H. Lee. Ann Arbor, MI: The Pierian Press, 1984, pp. 104-105.
13. Wilmer H. Baatz, "Collection Development in 19 Libraries of the Association of Research Libraries," *Library Acquisitions: Practice and Theory* 2 (1978):118-121.
14. Stanley P. Hodge, "Evaluating the Rate and Effectiveness of Approval Plans for Library Collection Development," in *Issues in Acquisitions: Programs and Evaluation*, edited by Sul. H. Lee. Ann Arbor, MI: The Pierian Press, p. 50.
15. Emery, op. cit., p. 194.
16. Daniel Melcher, *Melcher on Acquisition*. Chicago: American Library Association, 1971, p. 115.
17. *Approval Plans in ARL Libraries*. SPEC Kit 83. Washington, DC: Association of Research Libraries, Office of Management Studies, April 1982, pp. 59-60.

REFERENCES

Alessi, Dana L., "Coping with Library Needs: The Approval Vendor's Response/Responsibility." In Sul H. Lee, ed., *Issues in Acquisitions: Programs and Evaluation*, pp. 91-110. Ann Arbor, MI: The Pierian Press, 1984.
Approval Plans in ARL Libraries. SPEC Kit 83. Washington, DC: Association of Research Libraries, Office of Management Studies, April 1982.
Axford, H. William, "The Economics of a Domestic Approval Plan." *College and Research Libraries* 32 (1971):368-375.
Baatz, Wilmer H. "Collection Development in 19 Libraries of the Association of Research Libraries." *Library Acquisitions: Practice and Theory* 2 (1978):85-121.
Cargill, Jennifer & Alley, Brian, *Practical Approval Plan Management*. Phoenix: Oryx Press, 1979.
Conditt, Paul. "The Rise and Demise of Richard Abel and Company." *PNLA Quarterly* 39 (1975):10-14.
DeGennaro, Richard. "Escalating Journal Prices: Time to Fight Back." *American Libraries* 8 (1977):69-74.
DeVilbiss, Mary Lee, "The Approval-Built Collection in the Medium-Sized Academic Library." *College and Research Libraries* 36 (1975):487-92.
DeVolder, Arthur L., "Approval Plans—Bounty or Bedlam?" *Publishers Weekly* 202 (1972):18-20.
Dobbyn, Margaret, "Approval Plan Purchasing in Perspective." *College and Research Libraries* 33 (1972):480-84.
Downs, Robert B., "Collection Development for Academic Libraries: An Overview." *North Carolina Libraries* 34 (1976):31-38.
Dudley, Norman, "The Blanket Order." *Library Trends* 18 (1970):318-27.
Edelman, Hendrik, "Selection Methodology In Academic Libraries." *Library Resources and Technical Services* 23 (1979):33-38.
Emery, C. David, "Efficiency and Effectiveness: Approval Plans from a Management Perspective."

In Peter Spyers-Duran, ed., *Shaping Library Collections for the 1980s*, pp. 184-99. Phoenix, AZ: Oryx Press, 1980.
Evans, G. Edward & Argyres, Claudia White, "Approval Plans and Collection Development in Academic Libraries." *Library Resources and Technical Services* 18 (1974):35-50.
Feng, Y. T., "The Necessity for a Collection Development Policy Statement." *Library Resources and Technical Services* 23 (1979):39-44.
Ford, Stephen, *The Acquisition of Library Materials*. Rev. ed. Chicago: American Library Association, 1978.
Frye, Gloria & Romanansky, Marcia, "The Approval Plan—The Core of an Academic Wholesaler's Business." In Sul H. Lee, ed., *Issues in Acquisitions: Programs and Evaluation*, pp. 111-20. Ann Arbor, MI: The Pierian Press, 1984.
Futas, Elizabeth, ed., *Library Acquisition Policies and Procedures*. Phoenix, AZ: Oryx Press, 1977.
———, ed., *Library Acquisition Policies and Procedures*. 2d ed. Phoenix, AZ: Oryx Press, 1984.
Godden, Irene P., ed., *Library Technical Services: Operations and Management*. Orlando, FL: Academic Press, 1984.
Grant, Joan & Perelmuter, Susan. "Vendor Performance Evaluation." *Journal of Academic Librarianship* 4 (1978):366-67.
Grieder, Ted, *Acquisitions: Where, What, and How*. Westport, CT: Greenwood, 1978.
Harvey, John F. & Spyers-Duran, Peter, "The Effect of Inflation on Academic Libraries." In John F. Harvey and Peter Spyers-Duran, eds., *Austerity Management in Academic Libraries*, pp. 1-42, Metuchen, NJ: Scarecrow Press, 1984.
Hill, Bonnie Naifeh, "Collection Development: The Right and Responsibility of Librarians." *Journal of Academic Librarianship* 3 (1977):285-86.
Hitchcock-Mort, Karen, "Collection Management in the Eighties—Where Are We Now?" *Library Acquisitions: Practice and Theory* 9 (1985):3-12.
Hulbert, Linda Ann & Curry, David Stewart, "Evaluation of an Approval Plan." *College and Research Libraries* 39 (1978):485-91.
Jenks, George M., "Book Selection: An Approach for Small and Medium Sized Libraries." *College and Research Libraries* 33 (1972):28-30.
Lee, Sul H., ed., *Issues in Acquisitions: Programs and Evaluation*. Ann Arbor, MI: The Pierian Press, 1984.
Leonard, Lawrence E., Maier, Joan M. & Dougherty, Richard M., "Approval Plans and Centralized Processing." In their *Centralized Book Processing*, pp. 148-75. Metuchen, NJ: Scarecrow, 1969.
McCullough, Kathleen, "Approval Plans: Vendor Responsibility and Library Research: A Literature Survey and Discussion." *College and Research Libraries* 33 (1972):368-81.
———, Posey, Edwin D. & Pickett, Doyle C. *Approval Plans and Academic Libraries*. Phoenix, AZ: Oryx Press, 1977.
Maddox, Jane, "Approval Plans—Viable?" *Journal of Academic Librarianship* 1 (1976):22.
Magrill, Rose Mary & Rinehart, Constance, *Library Technical Service: A Selected, Annotated Bibliography*. Westport, CT: Greenwood, 1977.
——— & East, Mona. "Collection Development in Large University Libraries." In Michael H. Harris, ed., *Advances in Librarianship*, vol. 8, pp. 1-54. New York: Academic, 1978.
——— & Hickey, Doralyn J., *Acquisitions Management and Collection Development in Libraries*. Chicago: American Library Association, 1984.
Melcher, Daniel. *Melcher on Acquisitions*. Chicago: American Library Association, 1971.
Meyer, Betty J. & Demos, John T., "Acquisition Policy for University Libraries: Selection or Collection." *Library Resources and Technical Services* 14 (1970):395-99.
Newlin, Lyman W., "The Rise and Fall of Richard Abel and Co., Inc." *Scholarly Publishing* 7 (1975):55-61.
Osburn, Charles B., "Some Practical Observations on the Writing, Implementation, and Revision of Collection Policy." *Library Resources and Technical Services* 23 (1979):7-15.
Reidelbach, John H. & Shirk, Gary M., "Selecting an Approval Plan Vendor: A Step-by-Step Process." *Library Acquisitions: Practice and Theory* 7 (1983):115-22.
———, "Selecting an Approval Plan Vendor II: Comparative Vendor Data." *Library Acquisitions: Practice and Theory* 8 (1984):157-202.
———, "Selecting an Approval Plan Vendor III: Academic Librarians' Evaluations of Eight United States Approval Plan Vendors." *Library Acquisitions: Practice and Theory* 9 (1985):177-260.
Rouse, Roscoe, "Automation Stops Here: A Case for Man-Made Book Collections." *College and Research Libraries* 31 (1970):147-54

Schrift, Leonard, "After Thor, What's Next: The Thor Power Tool Decision (US Supreme Court) and Its Impact on Scholarly Publishing." *Library Acquisitions: Practices and Theory* 9 (1985):61-63.
Sewell, Robert G., "Managing European Automatic Acquisitions." *Library Resources and Technical Services* 27 (1983):397-405.
Spyers-Duran, Peter & Gore, Daniel, eds., *Advances in Understanding Approval and Gathering Plans in Academic Libraries*. Kalamazoo, MI: Western Michigan University, 1970.
_____, ed., *Approval and Gathering Plans in Academic Libraries*. Littleton, CO: Libraries Unlimited for Western Michigan University, 1969.
_____ & Gore, Daniel, eds., *Economics of Approval Plans*. Westport, CT: Greenwood, 1972.
_____ & Mann, Thomas, Jr., *Shaping Library Collections for the 1980s*. Phoenix, AZ:Oryx Press, 1980.
Wilden-Hart, Marion, "The Long-Term Effects of Approval Plans." *Library Resources and Technical Services* 14 (1970):400-406.

Truth in Vending

Leonard Schrift

When I first began contemplating the writing of this paper, I constantly returned to a simple fact: the bookseller is not the manufacturer of the book. The crucial role of the manufacturer which, in this case, happens to be the publisher deserves some attention before developing the real theme of my paper. In the book industry, the publisher is not only the manufacturer but he is also the one who determines and establishes prices, determines terms and conditions, and essentially dictates basic operating standards.

As an industry, book publishing is probably one of the least structured communities. It totally lacks any readily acknowledged standards and, although attempts by groups such as BISAC appear to be making some inroads, a quick examination of the players reveals that any embracing of these ideas is limited and fragmented at best. In addition, there is a general absence of uniformity and common business practice among publishers. It appears that each publisher is engaged in inventing his own "wheel," be it that of creating a totally computerized fulfillment system, developing returns and discount policy, or merely designing the shape and size of its invoices. Even a simple task such as title status codes, that so easily can be standardized across the industry, presents the recipients with a baffling array of codes and terms that vary from one publisher to the next. Not only do they vary, but, unfortunately, similar terminology may not necessarily indicate similarity of status from one publisher to the next.

When it comes to the crucial elements that determine the ultimate cost of the book: pricing, distribution, fulfillment, terms of supply and the like—the situation is even more chaotic and the absence of any real common practices and uniformity is even more evident.

The character of the industry was, and is, shaped by many forces. Historical developments, economic conditions, scientific and scholarly progress, technological innovations, all contribute to it. But, perhaps the most forceful and unique element that dulls true competition and enables each publisher to do his "own thing" is the protection granted by the copyright laws.

Historically, and until some twenty years ago, the driving force behind scholarly publishing had been the entrepreneurial scholar and bibliophile.

© 1987 by The Haworth Press, Inc. All rights reserved.

While attempting to be profitable, the publisher was mainly concerned with the editorial aspects of publishing. "Business sense," although desirable, took a back-seat to the sense of "mission" and the strong belief in the inherent importance of publishing scholarly works. As a result, publishers were willing to assume greater risks, and based their decisions more on the perception of the work's merit than on cold "bottom line" calculations.

However, in the last two decades the publishing industry has undergone thorough, profound changes that affect many aspects of its performance. In terms of ownership, many publishing houses were acquired by major corporations and conglomerates and transformed from scholarly-oriented enterprises to profit producing subsidiaries of entities, who may otherwise be completely divorced from any type of intellectual activity. The "intellectual glamor" associated with publishing and its inherently positive public perception might, in fact, have been the original motivation for conglomerates striving to gain a "socially positive" image. Such motivation was soon replaced by the "objective" and practical business considerations of maximizing profits, minimizing risks, and avoiding speculative ventures. Unavoidably, publishing style and character itself has subtly changed too, as publishing leadership has passed from the scholar and visionary entrepreneur into the hands of the "professional" manager.

It is a basic reality that books are not "products" in the mundane sense of the term, as only very insignificant value can be attributed to their physical properties. Being, in essence, a physical presentation of intellectual property, their true value is intangible and abstract. What then is the value of the book as a product? How is this value determined in monetary terms?

It would be a pleasure to describe a sensible and valid method used by publishers to establish prices. Unfortunately, such a method simply does not exist. A number of basic approaches are used by publishers and any number of combinations and permutations, thereof. One such approach is the "cost plus" method. It is based, essentially, on the estimated production costs, to which a variety of other cost elements are added in accordance with any number of formulas. Those elements are marketing, fulfillment, and overhead, as well as targeted profit margins. The total is divided by the number of units produced and BINGO!, the price is determined. Other publishers may refine this method to a higher degree and will price their books on a "per page" formula. Their life is uncomplicated. Simply estimate the number of pages, multiply it by the "per page" rate, and the price is established in an almost "scientific" way. Needless to say, publishers employing this approach are often faced with unpleasant surprises. The success of individual titles is not determined by the publisher's cost calculations, but rather by actual importance and value of the work, market conditions, effective promotion efforts, and other such factors that are being totally ignored. Many publishers take the exact opposite approach by basing the pricing of their books on the "whatever the market would bear" strategy. If a title is considered desirable, is expected to generate a demand, or "must" to libraries, a very high price is established, aimed at maximizing revenues rather than relating it to actual costs or achieving reasonable profit.

Still another approach employed by many publishers seems to alleviate the need for a pricing decision altogether. It is based on imitating or copying other publishers, particularly those deemed to be leaders in their fields. "This type of book is generally priced at 'X' price." "Similar books by X or Y publisher were priced at . . ." "X publisher did very well with similar titles selling it at . . ."

Like any other business, the publishing industry is subject to all forces operating in the general economic environment. The general increase in operating costs, production, and other such general overhead naturally exert upward pressure on prices.

The landmark Supreme Court decision eliminating the preferential treatment allowed publishers in valuing inventories initiated trends that altered traditional publishing wisdom in a very significant way. As a result, the reduction in the size of print runs raised the unit production costs which led to increases in list price. More important, it also cut the "in-print" life span of titles significantly and made reprinting even of successful titles less viable. Changes in ownership characteristics of many publishing companies also created upward pressure on prices. The now "publishing subsidiary" of the conglomerate is subject to new pressures to produce higher profits while, at the same time, it is forced to absorb higher and often unnecessary administrative and management charge allocations. Often being urged to reduce risks associated with speculative titles, publishers respond in paradoxical ways. Some reduce the scope and size of their publishing programs, while others publish a plethora of titles in "safe" subject areas causing an inevitable inundation of the discipline thus practically dooming the program to failure.

Establishing the list price, however, is only one aspect of the publisher's prerogatives as a manufacturer. The entire economic basis of the industry, be it publisher, bookseller or library, is determined by him. In addition to prices, the publisher determines all discounts, payment and prepayment terms, return policies, and ordering requirements. The problem is that, in all too many cases, such determinations are not a product of a logical process and common sense, but are completely arbitrary, ridden with idiosyncrasies, and lacking any resemblance of industry wide patterns. Ultimately, they all contribute to the final cost of the books. The publisher's stranglehold does not end, however, with direct money matters. On the nonmonetary plane, the publisher determines the effectiveness of fulfillment or lack thereof, the flow and accuracy of book information, the distribution of books, and ultimately their availability. The many shortcomings in these areas, too, add to the cost of the book.

The academic library bookseller is the essential link between the manufacturer—the publisher—and the consumer—the library. Perhaps the most important element in understanding the role of the bookseller is realizing that while his major function is providing the library with *service*, this service is expressed as a physical product—the book. Further, it is characterized by supply of single copies of a huge number of titles from thousands of sources. My purpose in making this point is not to tire you with stating the obvious, but, rather, to focus your attention on the realities of bookselling as a business.

To the bookseller, the basic cost of doing business represents a most significant element of the overall picture as it falls in the range of somewhere between 19 to 23 percent of total sales (in terms of the list price). The cost components are virtually identical to those that can be found in any business in any industry. The unique characteristics of bookselling determine, of course, the internal ratios of the individual cost elements.

The largest single cost element, comprising upward of 50 percent of the total operating and overhead expenses, is the cost of direct labor. The reasons for this high labor rate are easily understood when one considers that, by its very nature, bookselling is an extremely labor intensive operation. Although the academic bookseller deals in the course of a year with hundreds of thousands of books, each book must be handled individually, and each requires a high degree of manual input. Such input covers both clerical tasks through order processing, purchasing, invoicing, claiming and reporting; and physical handling through receiving, inspecting, shipment preparation, packing, and shipping activities.

Unfortunately, there is no practical way of reducing the amount of labor input required for the processing and handling of each individual order without injuring the quality of service in a major way. In fact, direct labor costs would be much greater if not for the incorporation of automation and computer technology. The extensive use of computerized systems has been the main contributor to the bookseller's success, so far, in checking the rise in labor cost while maintaining and enhancing his service capabilities.

The other 50 percent of the bookseller's operating and overhead costs are made up of the normal expenses necessary for the functioning of any business. The following partial listing illustrates the composition of such costs:

—*Statutory Employee Benefits*, such as: Social Security contributions, Workmen's Compensation Insurance, disability coverage.

— *Voluntary Employee Benefits*, such as: health insurance plans and retirement programs.
— *Space and Facilities Costs*, such as: rents or mortgage payments.
— *Utilities*, such as: electricity, heating, cooling, etc.
— *Communications Costs*, such as: telephone, telex, facsimile, on-line telecommunication costs.
— *Computer Hardware and Other Equipment*: costs of leasing, financing, maintenance contracts, etc.
— *Freight charges:* UPS, postage, motor freight, etc.
— *Supplies*: office supplies, computer supplies, packaging material, etc.
— *Travel and Meeting Costs*, such as: participation in library meetings and exhibits, professional conferences, traveling, and regional representatives, etc.

An additional, and very important, cost element relates to research and development activities. Although such activities may bear fruits only in the future, it is mandatory that important efforts and resources are dedicated to them on an on-going basis. The tasks of keeping pace with developments at the library, of assimilating new technologies, of refining and updating existing services, and of building new capabilites for the future are crucial to the very existence and survival of the bookseller.

These and other such business operating costs are always present and inescapable. Most of them are subject to incessant upward pressure and, in fact, often rise at a faster pace than the rate of inflation in the economy. Unfortunately, it is practically impossible to reduce them in any meaningful way, because the direct result of such reductions would be a parallel reduction in the level of service required by and provided to the library. As it is, every sort of managerial skill and technological capability is required for containing costs to the range of 19 to 23 percent of sales, cited by me earlier.

The bookseller's gross income is derived from the discounts granted him by the publishers. From my own experience, and from researching this issue in depth, I can state with a high degree of accuracy that the average discount enjoyed by the academic bookseller falls within the range of 29 to 32 percent. The exact positioning of the average within this range is determined in essence by three variables. The first of these is the actual "mix" of orders in terms of publishing sources. With the normal minor fluctuations, the bulk of titles supplied by academic library booksellers is from scholarly and scientific commercial publishers and university presses. On the fringes of the spectrum are scholarly trade titles from "trade" publishers on one hand, and noncommercial "esoteric" material from sources such as learned societies, associations, etc. on the other.

The second variable affecting the bookseller's relative average discount is his own size. With publishers, as with any other type of manufacturer, the size of the client does matter, and the major ones often benefit from a somewhat better negotiating position. The importance of this element should not be overestimated, yet it may, on occasion, be material nonetheless.

The third variable, however, the bookseller's relative purchasing efficiency, is quite important and can be very meaningful in its effect on the average discount received. As they do with most other aspects of their activities, publishers present booksellers with a maze of terms, conditions, plans, special situations, arrangements, etc. The ability of a bookseller to find his way in this maze is of extreme importance to achieving a more favorable level of discount. An endless number of considerations must be taken into account such as: subscribing to agency plans, ordering in minimum quantities, receiving automatic shipments, willingness to maintain certain inventory levels, participating in promotional schemes. The bookseller who is expert and efficient in his purchasing practices is likely to improve his average discount.

The ultimate cost to the library of monographic material is shaped therefore by rather definable parameters. Foremost, of course, is the list price established by the manufacturer—the publisher. The bookseller's own effect on the price is determined, on one hand, by the limitations on his gross income and, on the other hand, by the realities of his cost of operations.

The last important part needed to complete the picture is the discount received by the library. Numerous library studies, which my own experience supports, indicate that the average *overall* net discount enjoyed by academic libraries is somewhere between 6 percent and 9 percent, depending on their own particular "mix" of orders.

Subtracting the academic bookseller's 19-23 percent range of cost-of-doing business from his average discount range of 29-32 percent, will leave an amount of 6 to 13 percent to be divided between bookseller and library—13 percent under the most favorable conditions, 6 percent under the less favorable ones. The library's share is expressed by the discount it receives. The remainder is the bookseller's share, his profit.

My intention in presenting this analysis is not to depict the plight of the bookseller in terms of his narrow, and shrinking, profitability prospects. My purpose, rather, is to put into perspective the impact of economic reality on the pricing of monographs, and, just as importantly, to assess the future evolutionary prospects of the bookselling industry.

In this final segment of my paper, it seems appropriate to devote some thought to the future of booksellers. As we would all probably agree, any speculation on the future of bookselling is difficult, and, given all the elements and factors previously stated, there will be considerable room for argument. After discussions with several of my colleagues and having collected my own thoughts, I ostensibly drew a conclusion and would like to share with you the following prediction: Of the approximate twelve current academic library booksellers, I truly believe that over the course of the next six to ten years, that number will diminish to somewhere around six.[1] Although there are many more than twelve booksellers in the United States, certainly these twelve make up more than 90 percent of all academic library book sales. The likelihood is that collectively, the other seventy to eighty potential booksellers account for between 5 and 10 percent of the total potential sales.

There are many factors that will affect the bookselling community and ultimately reduce the size of the current ranks of the academic library wholesalers. Let me cite these factors and elaborate on them, as well as make several other points. First is acquisitions and mergers. We already have seen, and certainly will continue to see, the rather obvious cost effectiveness and benefit inherent in acquiring and/or merging of firms. Today, the prospect of sharing of resources, facilities, sales staff, travel expenses, as well as other significant costs is extremely attractive when two or more firms decide to merge with one another. Be it an acquisition or merger, this is a major factor which will lessen the choice of suppliers. Of the twelve booksellers, it would be the medium and smaller size firms in this group that would be primarily exposed to a takeover of sorts. The second factor, which probably will have a lesser impact but should nonetheless be pointed out, is that of failure. Although this is a subject we would all like to avoid discussing, including myself, it is inevitable that there will be failure at some time, an expectation that we must anticipate as well as accept. However, given the current financial condition of today's booksellers, the likelihood of one of the major wholesalers failing is extremely low. If a failure were to take place, it would probably occur with a smaller firm and, hopefully and probably, have a relatively little negative impact. Although I anticipate a certain degree of acquisitions and/or mergers, and perhaps some failures, what is really important is the lack of opportunity or, for that matter, interest for new booksellers to enter the community, by virtue of the same factors discouraging new players from developing a bookselling organization.

Of the factors cited here, the following are probably the most important. Factor number three is the extremely low profit margins. As I pointed out earlier in my paper, profitability is inherently low because of the huge number of small items carrying minimal profit margins. At any given time, any order placed by either library or bookseller will demonstrate that some 30 percent of the items ordered are not available (NYP, OS, NE, OP). This factor alone would probably discourage anyone from serious consideration of entering the field.

Factor number four is state-of-the-art technology requirements. Computerization and automation developments created a demand for a higher level of service. In terms of hardware and, more importantly, software and operating systems, it is a most costly proposition indeed. Further, this infrastructure requires years to develop, as it is evolutionary in nature and subject to continuous adjustments, modifications, and enhancements. The bookseller faces yet another expensive requirement in having to accommodate, cooperate, and interface with a plethora of individual libraries' systems and configurations.

This leads to factor number five, that besides the anticipation of low profit margins, a new organization today would require a rather large capital investment. Better return on such investments can be had much easier, and through lesser effort and risk, in other industries, or probably even through rather basic investing procedures. These capitalization prerequisites are needed in order to gain the capability to provide the sophisticated services already offered by firms existing in the market.

The final factor is the lack of available expertise. Other than a small number of individuals who are employed by existing organizations, and who might be opportunistic in desiring to begin their own organizations, there really exists no expertise outside of what is already in the industry. What I find most interesting is that perhaps ten or fifteen years ago one could begin a firm with a rather modest investment, limited publisher credibility, a few marketing skills, and simply grow into the market place. Today, in addition to the significant capitalization needed for the elements mentioned above, current working capital requirements are extremely high and prohibitive (labor intensive operations, inventory financing, tight credit policies by publishers, etc.). Several questions come to mind:

— What is the real future of booksellers?
— What will its role be?
— Who will be the survivors?

In order to lend support to my argument, I would like to use the following analogy: If we examine the community of periodical subscription agencies, we certainly must conclude that a major transition has taken place over the course of the last twenty years. At one time there were several dozen periodical sources serving libraries. Today, we find ourselves with two very predominant domestic agencies and, perhaps, two or three small to medium size specialists. The very reasons cited earlier as being factors that will effectively cause the decline in the rank of the booksellers, I identify in what has taken place over the last twenty years in subscription agencies. Further, and perhaps most decisively, in addition to the decline in the number of sources of supply, was the evolving change in the price of journal subscriptions to libraries. This aspect, too, has dramatically changed over the course of the last twenty years. At one time, although not conceivable by today's standards, discounts were offered by several agencies, a fact which today of course would be virtually unheard of. Today's current price not only includes payn·ent of the periodical subscription itself, but also includes a significant service charge. I do not intend to delve into the justification for service charges or discuss the periodical agent's cost of doing business. My purpose is to lend credence to my argument by drawing on the similarity of events and processes. In addition to all the factors cited earlier, the changes in pricing policy are attributed to a steady decline in discounts offered by publishers on their respective journals. This discount has shrunk to such an extent that in order for the agent to provide a meaningfully sophisticated computerized service, he is forced to add a service charge. There is already strong evidence among monographic scholarly publishers that this downward trend of discounts to booksellers has begun. I do not anticipate the complete elimination of discounts being offered by the booksellers, I do however feel that the discount, be it publisher's or bookseller's, will become a thing of the past over the next ten years.

Although I have painted a rather bleak picture of the future, I am truly optimistic and would very much like to end this paper on a positive note. The booksellers that will survive and exist ten years from now, in whatever shape or form, will be far superior to today's group. Of the six or so booksellers that will exist, each will be truly financially stable, each will have greater concentration of expertise, each will maintain state-of-the-art level of automation, and, finally, each will be capable of anticipating future library needs by being more responsive to the demands of the scholarly market place.

NOTE

1. John Secor, *Truth in Vending* (Paper delivered at Library Conference, Charleston, South Carolina, November 1985).

Books Across the Waters: An Examination of United Kingdom Monographic Pricing

Dana Alessi

"I never buy foreign books except for the occasional title the foreign language faculty request." As a representative for a United Kingdom firm, I hear this litany frequently chanted by librarians working in small to medium-sized libraries. Many of these librarians do not stop to consider that titles originally published in the U.K. but now available in the U.S. are, in actuality, "foreign" imprints. At the other extreme, librarians at research libraries may spend a significant percentage of the materials budget on British imprints, may utilize approval plans with a British vendor to bring in current U.K. materials, and may always order from the country of original publication. Regardless of the level of sophistication of the librarian, there is always a curiosity about the differences between U.K. and U.S. prices and why that difference exists.

Let us suppose a librarian is requested to purchase an Oxford University Press title. It is entirely likely that the title may be available in four separate forms—the original U.K. hardback, the U.K. paperback; the U.S. hardback, and the U.S. paperback. Four separate editions of the same title exist! Assuming the librarian decides to purchase the hardback, several more options exist:

1. Purchase the U.K. edition direct from Oxford University Press in England.
2. Purchase the U.K. edition from a library jobber in the U.K.
3. Purchase the U.S. edition from the U.S. branch or distributor of the original title.
4. Purchase the U.S. edition from a U.S. jobber.
5. Purchase from a local bookstore.

What is likely to be the most cost effective method of purchase for the library? A U.S. supplier is likely to supply the title at U.S. list price less a discount. The U.K. supplier will supply at U.K. list price plus a usual postage charge. Exchange rates must be factored if the title is purchased from the U.K. How can the librarian make an intelligent decision regarding the purchase of a U.K. title?

© 1987 by The Haworth Press, Inc. All rights reserved.

To provide a foundation for answering that question, I think it important to examine briefly the structure of the U.K. book trade and factors that influence pricing in the U.K. market.

In the U.S., the normal library purchasing relationships are, in order of importance, (1) library-jobber/wholesaler; (2) library-publisher; and (3) occasionally library-bookstore. In the U.K., the normal library purchasing relationships are (1) library-bookstore and (2) library-jobber/wholesaler. With the exception of seven regional DPO's, Direct Purchasing Organizations, which were established in the 1930s to buy textbooks and other school publications directly from publishers, only bookstores and jobbers/wholesalers buy directly from individual publishers. As Barry Fast has pointed out, this distribution arrangement among publishers, booksellers, and libraries is more formalized and organized than the U.S. method of distribution, since it clearly removes the publisher/manufacturer from the arena of direct competition with the booksellers whom they also supply for the ultimate consumer, whether it be library or individual. Thus, both bookseller and publisher are able to have a stable and equitable profit margin, contributing to the overall health of the book trade.[1]

The linchpin to the stability of the U.K. trade is the Net Book Agreement. Simply put, the Net Book Agreement prohibits a book from being sold by booksellers at less than the list price set by the publisher, with the exception of used books and books which have been held in the bookseller's stock for more than one year since the last purchase of the title. Libraries open to the public (i.e., public libraries and public academic institutions) are eligible to apply for a library license which allows them a 10 percent discount off net prices. All other libraries must purchase titles at the net price.

The Net Book Agreement has a long history worth reviewing briefly. The first documented instance of underselling occurred as early as the late eighteenth century when an enterprising bookseller realized he could get more customers and sell more books if he sold them cheaper than his competition.[2] Major publishers promptly attempted to boycott him. By 1829, a second attempt was made to stop underselling, and yet another effort failed in 1848.[3] During the succeeding four decades, discounting became rampant and gross profit margins shriveled to an average of 10 percent, driving many booksellers out of business.[4] Frederick Macmillan courageously published titles in the 1890s on a net basis, but his example was not widely followed.[5] After the formation of the London Booksellers' Society and the Associated Booksellers of Great Britain and Ireland in 1895 and the Publisher's Association in 1896, the latter initially opposing any attempt at resale price maintenance, a price agreement was finally hammered out, taking effect in 1900.[6] For over fifty years, this agreement remained in force.

In 1956, the Restrictive Practices Act was passed by Parliament. This act prevented manufacturers as a whole from prohibiting retailers to sell at less than the retail price, although individual enforcement was still permitted. A new Net Book Agreement came into force in 1957, which was duly brought for examination before the Restrictive Practices Court in 1962. The court allowed the Agreement to stand on the premise that "no two literary works are the same or alike in the way in which, or the extent to which, two oranges or two eggs may be said to be."[7] In other words, books are different. In addition, Justice Buckley reiterated the prime rationale for the Net Book Agreement—without the Net Book Agreement, there would be fewer stockholding bookshops with less variety of bookstock, resulting in a decline of publication and therefore higher prices. Bookstore profits were also judged to be modest in terms of profits of other business enterprises.[8]

Library and institutional sales account for approximately 20 percent of an average bookseller's volume in the U.K.[9] Thus, the library business is extremely important to booksellers, who are obviously interested in maintaining the integrity of the Net Book Agreement.

Booksellers operate differently in the U.K. in terms of stock. In the U.S., it is common for booksellers to buy large quantities of copies from publishers or wholesalers at deep discounts and to return them to publishers or to remainder them if they do not sell. In the U.K., booksellers hold titles purchased from publishers in stock, and the average stockholding bookstore will carry 10,000 titles.[10] Few titles are returned to publishers, and slow-selling titles may be sold at sale prices during the once a year National Book Sale. However, during the past several years, remainder shops have opened, and more returns to publishers have been allowed, marking somewhat of a change in attitude by publishers.

Discounts offered to booksellers by publishers rarely surpass 35 percent, except in the case of paperbacks, and technical title discounts average no more than 30 percent. The average discount to a bookseller runs between 30 and 35 percent, and quantity buying has no effect on discount given to a bookseller. Thus, if a bookseller buys four or forty copies, the discount will remain the same. If a bookseller purchases from a wholesaler, which can be more efficient in terms of turnaround for many titles, there is approximately a 5 percent sacrifice of discount. Single-copy orders usually carry a lower discount or a surcharge. Contrast this with the U.S. system of discount, where discounts increase based on numbers of copies purchased and are also based on type of book.

Although U.K. bookshops and libraries are significant to British publishers, of critical importance is the export market, particularly to English speaking countries such as the U.S., Canada, and Australia. The export market consistently accounts for approximately 40 percent of U.K. book sales,[11] compared with an average of no more than 8 percent for the U.S.[12]

To summarize then, there are four major areas of difference between

U.K. publishing and bookselling and U.S. publishing and bookselling—the Net Book Agreement, stockholding bookstores with strong backlist because of firm purchasing practices, library purchase from bookstores and wholesalers, rather than publishers and wholesalers, and the significance of the export market. All of these areas ultimately affect the pricing of a book to both the U.K. and U.S. market.

Because of the importance of the export market to U.K. bookselling, let us now turn to the ways in which a U.K. title can make its way across the Atlantic Ocean to the U.S. market for resale.

Before 1976, an edition of a title was usually either British or American, due to the British Publishers' Traditional Market Agreement.[13] The British Publishers' Traditional Market Agreement was a protocol formalized in 1947 but actually practiced long before that. Essentially, this agreement marked out territories where rights were required to remain in British hands, and generally included countries of the traditional British Empire. Certain markets were designated "open" markets where both countries could market different editions of the same title, but, in general, U.S. publishers would purchase rights from U.K. publishers for production of an American edition, and U.K. publishers would, in turn, purchase rights from U.S. publishers to print editions for the U.K. and countries covered by the Traditional Market Agreement. The Agreement was seen as an advantage to both U.K. and U.S. markets because (1) it kept the rights market healthy for U.S. publishers, since England was the largest market for foreign rights; (2) markets were not fragmented, thus providing for higher print runs and therefore lower unit costs; (3) foreign markets could best be served by the countries most familiar with those markets, resulting in maximized sales.[14]

However, during the early 1970s, the developing paperback industry, the rise of the international wholesaler, "buying around," and price and postage increases on the British market all contributed to put the Agreement in peril.[15] In 1974, the U.S. Department of Justice brought an antitrust suit against twenty-one U.S. publishers for conspiring to suppress competition and limit importation and exportation of books.[16] Although the case was never tried, a Consent Decree was signed in November, 1976, with the stipulation that, while rights could still be sold, territorial exclusivity could be negotiated only on a book basis.

Rights selling, the traditional method of getting a U.K. title to an American audience, is still very much alive and well, although the exclusivity of markets has almost disappeared. Occasionally, when ordering a title of U.K. origin from England, a library will be informed that it cannot be sold to the U.S. This is a vestige of the Traditional Market Agreement at work. It is particularly frustrating if the U.S. edition is no longer available.

Rights sales also benefit the author and "agents will continue to seek to sign separate contracts for the same titles in the U.K. and in the U.S., on the assumption that this is the way to maximize advance and royalty income for their clients."[17]

Rights contracts for a title originally published in the U.K. are usually negotiated in dollars. Depending on the exchange rate in force at the time of the rights sale, the ultimate price of the book can be affected, particularly if the dollar is strong against the pound.

Although rights sales are still common, two other methods of exporting have strengthened since the dissolution of the Traditional Market Agreement. The first of these is the true co-edition. Under this arrangement, two publishers, e.g., Grove and Macmillan, may agree to one printing of a title. For example, the text may be printed in the U.K. and the U.S. publisher may add his own title page and binding to the same text for the U.S. edition. For both publishers, there are definite economic advantages to be gained, since a longer print run may be produced, resulting in lower unit costs for both publishers. This is especially true in the academic market where a title may be so specialized it would be too expensive for one publisher to produce and promote; however, with the strength of two publishers sharing print costs, but each doing its own promotion, it becomes an economically viable production.

Because U.S. publishers were not always interested in purchasing rights and often demanded high discounts for co-editions, and because the Traditional Market Agreement no longer restricted British participation in the U.S. market, a third method of U.K. distribution gained additional favor in the late 1970s with establishment of more U.S. offices of U.K. publishers, not only for distribution but also for publishing. Additionally, other U.K. publishers contracted with publishers or distributors to promote and distribute their titles in the U.S.

Although it is faster to sell rights, co-publish, or contract for distribution, ultimately a U.K. publisher may achieve greater profitability by setting up his own office and doing his own distribution in the U.S. There is not the need for a rights sale; the publisher achieves the profits of sale in both the U.K. and the U.S. market, unlike a co-publishing agreement; and, by doing his own distribution, the publisher insures that his books are promoted in the fashion he likes and his list retains integrity. Obviously, the publisher also centralizes total price decision-making by having his own office.

Let's turn briefly to a discussion of how a U.K. publisher may set his U.S. price. First of all, in calculating a price, he must consider the unit cost of the book—such things as printing, paper, binding. Second, he must calculate the selling expenses for that title—marketing, promotion, and advertising. One publisher has estimated that "a modest mailing piece may cost 25¢ in direct costs; a catalog much more."[18] Also included might be the services of a direct mail list broker who will provide a current mailing list for catalog mailers, actually less expensive than if the publisher maintained his own list. In general, a publisher is likely to anticipate that 15 percent of a title's cost will be tied up in advertising and promotion. Also figured in must be about 20-25 percent for staff and overhead; a royalty to the author, usually around 10 percent; and warehousing and inventory expenses. Finally, a publisher must consider the type of book. Is it destined to be a trade title, an academic monograph, or a textbook? The title must be priced to fit the market. A trade title, appealing to the general public, usually begins to meet price resistance if priced much above $24.95, and the bulk of trade titles will be priced in the $10.95-$19.95 range. Academic monographs, depending on subject matter, are usually priced between $24.95 and $45.00, with sci-tech titles commanding significantly higher prices. It is logical to assume that smaller print runs and therefore higher unit costs result in higher priced academic monographs. Textbooks will usually be priced in the $15.95 to $19.95 range, if paperback, and hard cover textbooks around $30.00. Ideally, the publisher will price for the market and will price competitively with that market. If the average sociology monograph costs $30.00, it will probably not make much economic sense for a publisher to price his sociology monograph at $65.00 unless unit costs dictate.

The exchange rate is also considered. Pricing according to the going exchange rate is risky; a publisher must engage in speculation as to what the exchange rate will be by the time his book is published in the U.S. edition, often several months in the future. The usual practice is to take the going exchange rate and inflate about 25-33 percent. Thus, with a current exchange rate of dollar to pound at about $1.48, multiplying the U.K. price by two is a common practice. With luck, that will cover the unit cost, advertising and promotion, staff, royalties, and overhead; will price for the market; and will still allow a healthy margin of profit.

Thus, a picture begins to emerge of reasons for price disparity for the U.S. and U.K. editions of a title. If a title has taken the rights route, each publisher is free to set his own price. The price is figured on each publisher's costs, and the exchange rate may have little or no bearing. Co-published titles may have similar prices, based on exchange rates at time of co-publication, but subject to price differentials as exchange rates fluctuate. Distributed titles may reflect the publisher's decision of pricing for the U.S. market, but, by doing his own promoting and distribution from his own office, a publisher is free to set his own U.S. price regardless of the U.K. price. Depending upon how the publisher views the U.S. market and how sagacious he is, he may set the price too low, about right, or unfairly high to take advantage of the U.S. export market.

Because of the uncertainties of U.S. versus U.K. pricing, many librarians find it easier to order all titles from a U.K. supplier. By ordering U.K. titles from a U.K. supplier, what can the librarian expect in terms of costs?

First, all titles will be billed at the U.K. list price per the provisions of the Net Book Agreement. In January, 1983, the American Library Association Resources and Technical Services Division Executive Board passed a resolution supporting the right of U.S. libraries to apply for a library license so that the 10 percent discount extended to U.K. libraries could be offered to U.S. libraries also. In June, 1983, Charles Willett of the University of Florida applied to the Publishers' Association for a library license for his library. After careful and deliberate consideration by the Publishers' Council, Mr. Willett's application was denied on the basis that library licensing applied only to libraries in the U.K. and that by allowing U.S. libraries to purchase at a discount in the U.K., the export market could be hurt.[19] Thus, net pricing remains in effect for U.S. libraries. If a supplier would supply to U.S. libraries at a discount, he risks the wrath of the powerful Publishers' Association, whose members could simply refuse to supply the renegade with titles needed.

Second, as most U.K. suppliers invoice in U.S. dollars, a conversion of the U.K. list price, either on a line by line basis or sum total basis, will have been calculated. If a librarian checks the *Wall Street Journal* to compare conversion rates on the date of invoice, he/she will almost always find a discrepancy of a few cents. U.K. suppliers to the U.S. library market will normally consult their bankers on a daily or weekly basis for the official "buying" rate—in other words, how many dollars would it take to *buy* £1 sterling. The rate quoted in the *Wall Street Journal* is the spot rate, i.e., the middle rate between buying and selling. Thus, an invoice will always have a slight discrepancy in what seems to be the vendor's favor but in actuality is the buying rate.

Obviously, if one is purchasing from the U.K., exchange rates must be watched carefully. An analysis of exchange rates in January and June of each year since 1978 reflects a British pound worth $1.91 on January 1, 1978, and $1.47 on January 1, 1986. Within that eight-year period, the pound has ranged from a low of $1.19 in January, 1985, to a high of $2.44 in June, 1980, and January, 1981.[20] Thus, a book costing £10 would have been priced to the U.S. library market, depending on time of purchase, anywhere from $11.90 to $24.40—or over a 200 percent differential! However, even in 1980 and 1981, the average U.K. title still maintained a price advantage over its U.S. counterpart because of pricing considerations for the U.S. market which have previously been discussed.

Third, most U.S. libraries will pay the freight charges from their U.K. suppliers. There are essentially three methods of shipping from the U.K.: sea mail, which is inexpensive but slow; air mail, which is fast but expensive; and accelerated surface post. Accelerated surface post (ASP) utilizes the normal internal surface mail systems in the U.S. and U.K. but air between the two. Price falls between surface mail and air mail.

The average postage charge to the library will be around 5 percent of invoice total. What does the library get for this 5 percent? Assuming shipment ASP, it receives posting from the point of origin to the air cargo carrier; shipment by air to the U.S.; the services of a customs broker engaged by the U.K. supplier to clear customs at the U.S. destination; transport to the next point of shipment; the agents' fee for reposting reshipment through the U.S. mail, and the U.S. actual mail costs. Compare that charge and that service to the usual U.S. jobber transportation charge of 3-4 percent, and it can be seen that shipment rates from the U.K. are bargains.

An ominous threat looms on the horizon, however. The U.K. Post Office raised overseas postage rates significantly in November 1985. Surface consolidation items increased by 100 percent, accelerated surface post by 57 percent for items under 60 grams. Although the overall banding discount on ASP and bulk airmail did increase by 1p per kilo, direct agents' bags increased by 21 percent and the printed papers reduced rate by 20 percent. Further postage hikes are expected, even though the U.K. Post Office makes a significant profit from overseas mail.[21] Needless to say, U.K. suppliers are exploring other methods of shipment.

One further comment should be made about shipping. All printed books, microforms, maps, charts, etc., enter the U.S. on a duty-free basis according to the provisions of the Florence Agreement.[22] The Florence Agreement also prohibits discriminatory taxation on books and microforms. Thus, even if the U.K. were to decide to impose the VAT (value-added tax) on books produced in the U.K. (as there has recently been a threat to do), the Florence Agreement should prohibit this tax from being passed on to U.S. libraries. Sixty-eight countries now subscribe to the Florence Agreement, approved by the UNESCO General Conference in 1950 to facilitate the free flow of educational, scientific, and cultural materials.[23]

The librarian wondering whether to purchase the U.K. or U.S. edition of that Oxford University Press title mentioned at the beginning of this paper may now have a more solid foundation on which to make a sound decision for purchase on the basis of the points I have briefly outlined. The general evidence, however, points to the advantages of purchasing from the country of original publication. One's overall costs should be lower, even purchasing at list price.

Unfortunately, there is little solid information in the library literature regarding prices for British academic books that a librarian can use with authority for making budgeting and purchasing decisions. And yet, this is the final piece of information which the librarian needs to make an intelligent purchasing decision.

Average book prices in issues of *The Bookseller* include too many popular and public library titles to be meaningful. Prices for British books as reported in the *Bowker Annual,* which are collected by the

Loughborough University of Technology Centre for Library and Information Management (CLAIM) are based on copyright books deposited in the Cambridge University Library. But, because the British National Bibliography increasingly is printing either CIP information without prices or full bibliographic citations for previous year imprints, it is no longer a reliable source for compilation of information.[24] The RTSD Library Materials Price Index Committee is working with the price information for new British books supplied on approval from B. H. Blackwell in the hopes that this information may prove more reliable.[25] Additionally, Draft Proposal 9230 — Criteria for Price Indexes for Library Materials — is currently being circulated for approval or disapproval to members of the National Information Standards Organization (Z39) International Committee. This proposal, in process since 1983, parallels the U.S. standard, but addresses specifically price indexes for international materials and recommends use of the UNESCO subject breakdown for consistency.[26]

Ultimately, with greater knowledge of the U.K. publishing scene and its relationship to libraries and booksellers, with further insight into pricing by U.K. publishers to the domestic and international market, with better understanding on how exchange rates fluctuate and are set and how postage is determined, and with more reliable price studies and indexes, a librarian may more comfortably acquire those "books across the waters" and know that he/she has made the proper purchasing decision and wisely expended his/her library funds.

NOTES

1. Barry Fast, "Publishing and Bookselling; a Look at Some Idiosyncrasies," *Library Acquisitions: Practice and Theory*, 3 (1979):16.
2. Russi Jal Taraporevala, *Competition and Its Control in the British Book Trade, 1850-1939* (London: Pitman Publishing, 1973), pp. 14-15.
3. Ibid., p. 17.
4. Ibid., pp. 24-27.
5. Ibid., pp. 34-35.
6. Ibid., pp. 40-46.
7. Ian Norrie, *Mumby's Publishing and Bookselling in the Twentieth Century*, 6th ed. (London: Bell & Hyman, 1982), pp. 168-69. For a full report of the defense of the Net Book Agreement, including extended testimony, see the monumental R. E. Barber and G. R. Davies, *Books Are Different* (London: Macmillan; New York: St. Martin's, 1966).
8. Ibid.
9. Peter J. Curwen, *The UK Publishing Industry* (Oxford: Pergamon Press, 1981), p. 99.
10. Ibid., p. 42
11. The 40 percent is widely acknowledged to be the standard figure. See Jeremy Booth, "Rationalization and Crisis: a Quarter Century of British Publishing," in *Perspectives on Publishing*, eds. Philip G. Altbach and Sheila McVey (Lexington: Lexington Books, 1976) p. 63; Norrie, *Mumby's Publishing and Bookselling*, p. 223; Curwen, *The UK Publishing Industry*, pp. 8-9; Ion Trewin, "British Publishing: Many Troubles, Some Reasons for Cheer," *Publishers' Weekly*, 17 September 1979, pp. 111-12.
12. *The Bowker Annual of Library and Book Trade Information*, 30th ed., ed. and comp. by Julia Moore (New York: Bowker, 1985), p. 472.
13. Mary Nell Bryant, "English Language Publication and the British Traditional Market Agree-

ment," *Library Quarterly*, 49 (1979):371-98, provides an excellent summary of the agreement, its background and subsequent demise and implications. See also Gordon Graham, "After the Consent Decree: a New Era in the Marketing of English-Language Books," *Publisher's Weekly*, 31 January 1977, pp. 38-40.

14. Bryant, "English Language Publications," pp. 377-78.
15. Ibid., pp. 378-80.
16. Ibid., p. 373.
17. Graham, "After the Consent Decree," p. 38.
18. Robert Leider, "How Librarians Help Inflate the Price of Books," *American Libraries*, 11 (1980):559.
19. For a full account of the correspondence between Charles Willett and the Publishers' Council, see Charles Willett and Peter Phelan, "The Willett-Phelan Letters," *Library Acquisitions: Practice and Theory*, 9 (1985):169-76.
20. See Appendix for U.S. dollar/British pound exchange rates from 1978-1986.
21. "Post Office Price Inflation Will Damage Publishers and Printers," *The Bookseller*, 26 October 1985, p. 1723.
22. "Delegates Adopt Protocol for Florence Agreement," *Publishers' Weekly*, 26 April 1976, pp. 20-21.
23. Robert W. Frase, "Will International Duties Be Removed on A-V Materials and Microforms?" *Publisher's Weekly*, 20 October 1975, pp. 41-42.
24. *Bowker Annual*, p. 475.
25. Christopher Tyzack, 1986, personal communication.
26. Frederick Lynden to Alessi, 31 January 1986.

APPENDIX

British £ Sterling/U.S. Dollar Exchange Rates
January, 1978-January, 1986

January 1, 1978	$1.91
June 1, 1978	$1.88
January 1, 1979	$2.10
June 1, 1979	$2.11
January 1, 1980	$2.28
June 1, 1980	$2.44
January 1, 1981	$2.44
June 1, 1981	$2.12
January 1, 1982	$1.90
June 1, 1982	$1.84
January 1, 1983	$1.57
June 1, 1983	$1.60
January 1, 1984	$1.48
June 1, 1984	$1.44
January 1, 1985	$1.19
June 1, 1985	$1.34
January 1, 1986	$1.47

Mountains and Molehills: How University Presses Determine Book Prices and How Those Prices Relate to Library Budgets

George W. Bauer

Later in this paper mountains and molehills will be used in something approximating their usual context. At the outset, however, I use them to contrast the mountainously high prices of some specialized scholarly books with the pathetically small piles of money available for their purchase in many academic libraries. Both aspects of that perception are a matter of perspective, of course. As a responsible scholarly publisher I know that even when the price I set for a large and specialized work is high enough to cause a certain degree of vertigo, it is nonetheless far below the book's true value. More precisely, the list price almost invariably is too low to provide adequate compensation for the actual costs incurred in publishing the book. The larger and more expensive the project, the higher the probability that the price, breathtaking though it may be, has been reduced through the application of a subvention to offset, or at least reduce, the losses that would otherwise be incurred in the myriad activities that transform a manuscript into a book and ultimately get it into the hands of readers: editing and designing; typesetting, printing, and binding; marketing, invoicing, and shipping, to name only the most obvious.

As one example from the recent University of Oklahoma Press list let me cite *The Papers of Chief John Ross*, edited by Gary E. Moulton. Its two volumes, totalling more than 1600 pages, present almost 1200 letters, speeches, and other documents written by Ross, who was principal chief of the Cherokees for nearly 40 years and served the tribe in a public capacity for more than five decades spanning the tribe's removal from the southeastern United States and their resettlement in what is now Oklahoma. At $95.00 per set, these books are among the most expensive items on our list. Yet without a substantial subvention from the National Historical Publications and Records Commission of the National Archives, which also underwrote research for the volumes, the price would have had to be more than $125.00. Indeed, the Press could not have undertaken this major project at all without such support, which brought both the publishing risk and the immediate outlay of cash within manageable parameters, in part by allowing us to set a high but, we hope, acceptable price.

The molehill of available funds for book purchase is also a matter of perception, and those of you involved in library acquisitions must live daily with the reality of limited budgets. As a scholarly publisher involved almost entirely with books rather than journals I am chagrined to see the results of surveys like a recent study conducted by John P. Dessauer for the Professional and Scholarly Publishing Division of the Association of American Publishers on the acquisition of books by academic libraries,[1] which shows that only about one-sixth of the materials budget of the responding libraries is devoted to book purchases.

A central fact of library budgets is the labor-intensive nature of library operations, a characteristic also of university presses and of higher education as a whole. A decade or so ago an economist on the staff of the American Council on Education, speaking at an annual meeting of the Association of American University Presses, pointed out an anomalous situation facing all institutions of higher learning. Although in theory they are tax exempt as well as not-for-profit, they are not excused from contributing payroll taxes. Because such a high proportion of their total budget is devoted to salaries and wages, they may actually carry a proportionately larger tax burden than does a capital-intensive manufacturer earning substantial profits. You might share that intriguing thought with research librarians and faculty members at your university and encourage them to suggest the topic to a student looking for a research project. Given the dramatic increase in Social Security taxes over the past decade, it would be enlightening to see comparisons of the total tax burdens borne by universities and industrial concerns.

Anyone seeking an understanding of how a publisher approaches the economics of a single book could hardly do better than to read Chapter IV of *The Art and Science of Book Publishing*, by Herbert S. Bailey, Jr., Director of Princeton University Press.[2] Bailey devotes "particular attention to the determination of the print order, the price, the discount, the royalty rate, and the budget for operating costs related to the book." He develops algebraic formulas but adds that the use of mathematics "should not be allowed to give a false impression of precision in an area where judgment is essential and estimates are necessarily imprecise." Please keep that caution in mind while reading my comments on how university presses determine book prices.

The most direct method I know for relating the production cost of a book to the list price needed to cover all publishing costs was worked out in 1969 by Roger McCarthy, then a colleague of mine at Cornell University Press. As assistant director of the Press for 15 years, I was involved in the pricing of new books and reprints. The basic approach to pricing, which I had learned many years earlier, involved use of a rule of thumb to arrive at a first approximation of the list price that, for a given combination of discount and royalty, would produce the desired contribution to the Press's operating expenses. The fine tuning that followed often required working out three or four sets of computations. Before electronic calculators became the norm, the computations could be worked out with a mechanical calculator, clacking endlessly with each multiplication or division, or worked out with pencil and paper. For each combination of production cost and royalty terms it could easily take ten minutes to determine the target price, the list price coming closest to achieving the desired gross margin.

Becoming increasingly irritated with the inefficiency of that approach to pricing, I started casting about for a more direct method. There must be a multiplier, I became convinced, that could be applied to the production cost of each book in order to produce exactly the list price required. To test the idea I began comparing the production costs and list prices of recently published books in the same discount category and with the same royalty terms. As I expected, dividing the production costs into the list prices produced a set of closely similar figures. I had completed half a dozen computations when Roger McCarthy arrived at my office for our regular weekly meeting, so I explained what I was doing and asked Roger to give some thought to the problem. The very next morning he came back to me with a solution that is positively elegant in the mathematical sense, a solution that I call the McCarthy Method.

Before explaining the method, I need to set the stage briefly. If a publisher is to set prices rationally, he must first determine the net income required to cover all expenses, including production costs, royalties, operating expenses, and, if his is a commercial venture, a profit margin. The operating expenses can be subdivided in any way the publisher sees fit, and it is not unusual for a firm to account specifically for editorial, design, and marketing costs as separate items. For the purposes of this paper, however, I will take the simplest possible approach and say that only three elements must be accounted for: production costs, royalties, and operating expenses or overhead. Working with those elements, Roger McCarthy explained his pricing method in these terms:

Let the list price of a book equal 100 percent. Then subtract whatever percentages are needed to cover discounts, royalties, and the publisher's operating expenses. The remainder can be applied to cover production costs. When the percentage of list price necessary to cover production cost is expressed as a decimal, dividing the unit production cost by that factor gives the precise list price that will produce sufficient revenues to cover discounts, royalties, production costs, and the targeted allowance for general overhead.

Because words tend to obscure the simplicity of the method, let me present an example. In order to allow the reader to compare the McCarthy Method with an algebraic expression of the gross margin pricing formula, I will draw the figures from an excellent article by Colin Day entitled "The Theory of Gross Margin Pricing."[3] Day made the following assumptions: that the average discount is 30 percent, that the royalty rate is 10 percent of list price, and that the target gross margin is 55 percent of actual income. Expressing these figures in decimal form, we have:

Average discount	.30	
Royalty	.10	
Target gross margin	.385	(the net sales income of .70 × target gross margin percentage, .55)
Total	.785	

Subtracting .785 from 1.000 yields .215 as the appropriate factor for calculating the list price. If the unit production cost is $5.786, as in Day's example, dividing that figure by .215 yields a list price of $26.91. Not surprisingly, that price is the same one Day arrives at.

To take full advantage of the McCarthy Method a publisher should first chart all the royalty percentages he uses along with the corresponding divisors. Assuming an average discount of 30 percent and a target gross margin of 55 percent, the chart would look like this:

TABLE 1

Royalty	Pricing Factor
Waived	.315
10% of net income after discount	.245
10% of list price	.215
12.5% of list price	.19
15% of list price	.165

If royalty terms have already been decided, an editor confronted with an estimate showing unit costs for three possible print quantities can simply divide the unit cost for each quantity by the appropriate pricing factor in order to determine the minimum list prices that would produce the desired gross margin. If, however, the royalty has not yet been determined, he can quickly work out the formula prices for various combinations of print quantity and royalty level. Each computation takes only a few seconds on a calculator, and of course the pricing factors can easily be programmed into a computer.

The McCarthy Method becomes even more valuable when the table of royalties and pricing factors is expanded to cover all discount categories used by the publisher. Presumably the average discount of 30 percent shown in Table 1 represents short-discount titles. Let us add a column for trade-discount titles, applying the assumption that the average discount for such titles is 43 percent. The resulting chart of pricing factors is shown in Table 2.

Using these pricing factors, an editor assigned to recommend royalty terms as well as print quantity and price can calculate half a dozen or more alternatives in less time than most of us would require to work through the algebraic formula for a single combination of unit cost and royalty.

The McCarthy Method is the most direct approach I know for calculating prices that would provide the desired allowance for operating expenses. Clearly, however, it does not substitute for the publisher's judgment as to what constitutes an acceptable price for a given book. The target price may, in the publisher's judgment, be unreasonably high. Perhaps it will then be necessary to seek a subvention in order to lower the price to an acceptable level. In rare instances the target price may seem lower than the norm for comparable books, allowing the publisher to set a higher price and apply the surplus income toward covering losses incurred on other titles.

The McCarthy Method shows us how, given the unit production cost of a book, to calculate the break-even price. To approach an understanding

TABLE 2

Royalty	Pricing Factors	
	Short-Discount Titles	Trade-Discount Titles
Waived	.315	.256
10% of net income after discount	.245	.199
10% of list price	.215	.156
12.5% of list price	.19	.131
15% of list price	.165	.106

of book pricing, however, and particularly to comprehend why some book prices have risen much more sharply than others, we need to explore other factors. Why do two books of essentially the same size and typographical complexity, perhaps both coming from the same university press, carry widely differing prices? The answer may be found in the size of the print run, and therein lies a sad tale. The costs of carrying a book from manuscript to the point of being ready to start the printing presses—setting, proofing, and correcting the type; pasting up the pages and photographing them; making the printing plates and adjusting them on the presses—are substantially the same whether the publisher is going to print 3000 copies or 1000 copies. Let us assume that those costs total $7,500, a plausible figure for a typical book of 320 pages. For a run of 3000 copies the publisher's investment in those fixed costs represents $2.50 per copy, but if the run is reduced to 1000 copies the investment per copy leaps to $7.50. And the sad reality is that unit sales of scholarly books, and therefore the feasible print quantities, have been dropping for more than a decade.

The trend is succinctly summarized by the largest of the university presses, the University of Chicago Press, in its successful application to the National Endowment for the Humanities, filed in May 1983, for a challenge grant. The press reported, "In 1973, we routinely printed 2,000 to 3,000 copies of each new specialized monograph; in 1975, a sales study proved that we should print only 1500 copies of new monographs; in 1978 we saw that the average five-year sales of scholarly works had dropped to approximately 1,000 copies." Their application went on to say, "It is clear that the market for books in the humanities has contracted. Books that receive magnificent scholarly reviews may sell as few as 700 copies in the first three years." At the University of Oklahoma Press our experience is very much the same. Despite receiving excellent reviews and even winning significant prizes, our specialized books often fail to achieve sales as high as 1,000 copies in the first three years. What used to be mountains of sales, relatively speaking, have become molehills. Inevitably the reduced sales are reflected in shorter print runs, which in turn lead to higher prices and further restrict purchases from the limited funds available to academic libraries.

NOTES

1. *Library Acquisition Survey*, Scranton, PA: Center for Book Research, University of Scranton, 1985.
2. New York: Harper & Row, Publishers, 1970; paperback edition, Austin, TX: University of Texas Press, 1980.
3. *Scholarly Publishing*, July, 1983, pp. 308-309. Day also presents a thoughtful critique of the shortcomings of the gross margin pricing method and suggests an alternate approach.

Acquisitions Costs:
How the Selection of a Purchasing Source Affects the Cost of Processing Materials

Edna Laughrey

The cost of materials added to library collections should be thought of in broader terms than simply the amount paid for the materials acquired. The real cost of materials added to library collections must include the expenditures for staff, space, supplies and systems. Library materials go through a processing function before they are readily available to patrons. These costs must be considered when determining the actual cost of adding materials to library collections.

The source of purchase is another factor to consider when reviewing the total cost of library materials. Cataloging and circulation costs may not be affected by the source of purchase, but the acquisitions costs are greatly affected by this decision. Indeed, how materials are acquired may be the largest single influence on acquisition costs. Acquisitions librarians sometimes neglect to consider internal processing costs when making the decision of where materials should be ordered. We are often unaware of the difference in costs of ordering materials directly from the publisher or through booksellers, middlemen, wholesalers or vendors. We must begin to consider those financial differences. For this paper the term vendor will be used to represent booksellers, wholesalers, or middlemen.

The University of Michigan Library system purchases some 60,000 volumes a year and spends close to four million dollars for those materials. The materials are purchased world-wide and are chiefly single copies of short-discount, scholarly or technical books.

We at the University of Michigan Library did a retrospective study of our ordering patterns and the resulting workloads. We compiled statistics of orders placed with publishers and those ordered through vendors. The study was limited to orders for paper products, excluding serial standing orders and subscriptions, microforms, scores, recordings and the like. We limited the study to domestic monographs and the remainder of the paper will review those results. They will vividly portray the vendor as the less expensive source for fulfilling the orders of a large academic library.

We began the study by reviewing all the firm orders placed or materials accepted on approval plans on two days in each of twelve months. The sample size was 2,365. We have found that for overall savings and maximum fulfillment rate, vendors are preferable to publishers as a purchasing source. Significant internal savings can be verified by a step by step examination of the library acquisition process.

ORDERING

Roughly half of the domestic materials we acquire come on approval plans as illustrated in Figure 1. Of the remaining half, the firm orders, 43.2% are received as the result of orders placed with vendors and 6.5% of orders are placed directly with publishers. We found that the 6.5% of titles ordered directly from publishers accounted for 43.5% of the total pieces of mail we needed to send to suppliers. The 43.2% of the orders placed with vendors account for 34.8% of the pieces of mail. Of the 50.3% of the materials arriving on approval, 30.5% come as books and do not require purchase orders. The other 19.8% are the result of form selections or offers and account for 21.7% of the pieces of mail.

When orders are printed they are sorted by purchasing source and stuffed in envelopes for mailing. This process takes place on a daily basis. Firm orders to vendors account for a relatively large number of orders being placed with a relatively few sources. Conversely, direct orders to publishers, result in relatively few titles coming in from a large number of sources. As we proceed, you will come to see the impact of this difference on our processing costs.

Another way to look at the differences being described is to think about the degree of supplier concentration in each of the three ordering categories. The first two columns of Figure 2 show that a very few suppliers for approval and firm orders account for all materials received in this way. We took all 2,365 items in the study and sorted them by publisher. The result of that sort is the column listed as publisher. That column reflects how many materials would be received from each publisher were we to go directly to the publisher for all the titles in the sample. The publisher receiving the largest number of orders would have accounted for only 2.5% of the titles in the sample. The top five publishers combined account for only 10.9% of the total orders. Without vendors, we would have been dealing with 645 different suppliers to acquire the 2,365 titles in our sample. By far, the greatest majority of these publishers would have provided us with a single volume.

PRE-CODING

Within our workflow, the ordering process involves some pre-coding of order slips before title information is input into our automated acquisitions system. All orders are assigned to a fund, the cataloging location is

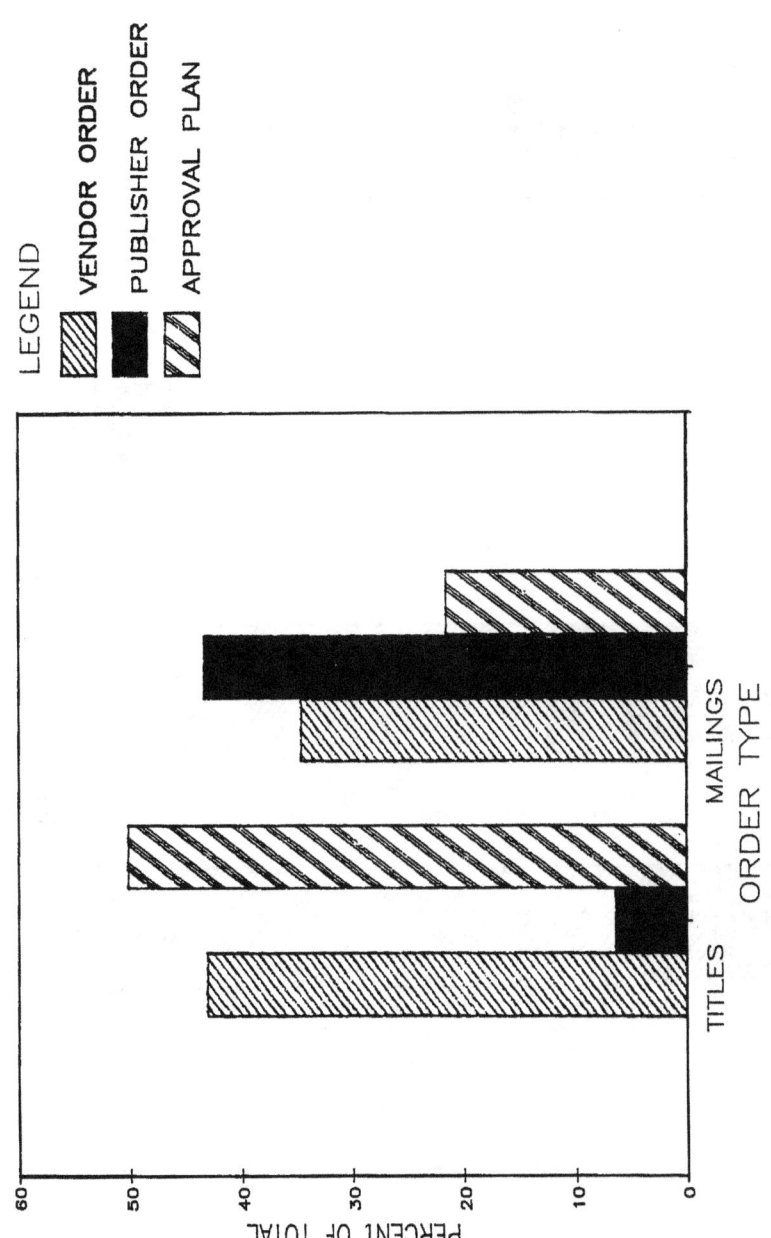

FIGURE 1. Titles Ordered and Resulting Pieces of Mail

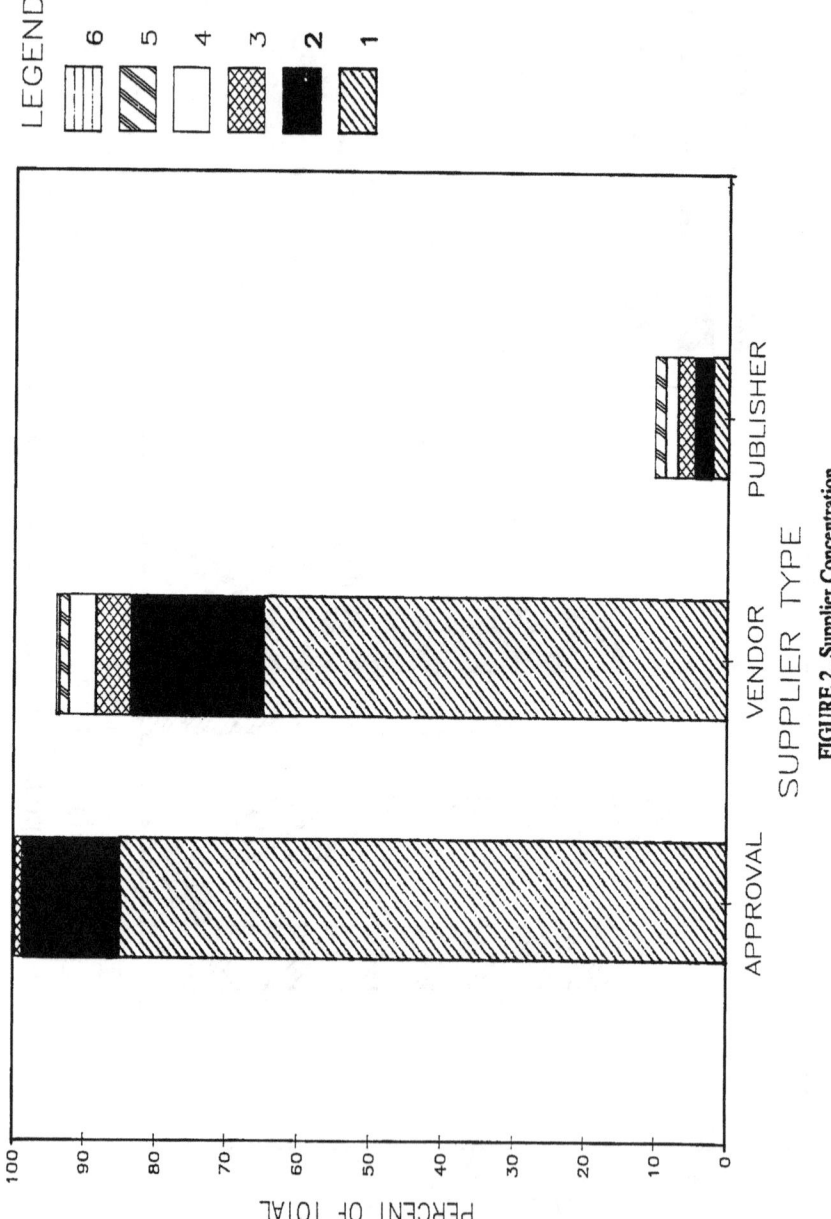

FIGURE 2. Supplier Concentration

indicated, and a vendor code is identified. Once input, the vendor code which ranges from one to five characters will cause a proper mailing address to appear on printed order slips. If we were to order all materials directly from the publisher, the large number of publishers with whom we would deal would make it impractical to maintain a computer-linked file of their addresses.

Generally, the requests we receive to order materials do not include publisher addresses. If we were to order those materials directly from the publisher it would be necessary for the person who pre-codes orders to look up and write out the full mailing address of publishers for each direct order. We estimate that this involves an average of 2.5 minutes per order with times ranging from one to 15 minutes. Figure 3 shows the difference in time for coding the average order for a vendor, 1.2 minutes, and an order where the publisher address was not in the automated system, 3.7 minutes. It is obviously a time-savings for us to have codes for the system that explode to full addresses rather than needing to hunt for and code the publisher specific name and address. If all materials in the study were coded for vendors the coding time would have amounted to 2,838 minutes or 47.3 hours. Conversely, if all the orders had gone directly to publishers the result would be 8,750 minutes or 145.8 hours.

INPUTTING

Ordering materials has been greatly facilitated by the advent of computerized acquisitions systems. Data are readily entered, stored and retrieved to permit access to a broad range of information about materials acquisitions. In the case of the acquisitions system we use, most of the costs associated with the system were incurred at the time of purchase. Ongoing expenses are primarily represented by the labor cost of data entry. It is therefore desirable that we optimize speed of entry while maintaining a constant standard of accuracy.

It is very difficult to generalize about the rate at which we input orders. There is a fair amount of variation from individual to individual and then again by the nature of the material being entered. Overall, it would seem that 2.6 minutes per unit represents a fair average for inputting time.

Inputting direct orders to publishers involves a fairly substantial time increment because the system requires that each mailing address not already coded in the vendor file be keyed in for each item. This is true even when multiple orders are being sent to the same publisher. There is a great deal of variation in the time required for this procedure but a fair estimate would appear to be 45 seconds or a 30% increase over the base average for inputting a record. Figure 3 shows inputting for vendor coded orders

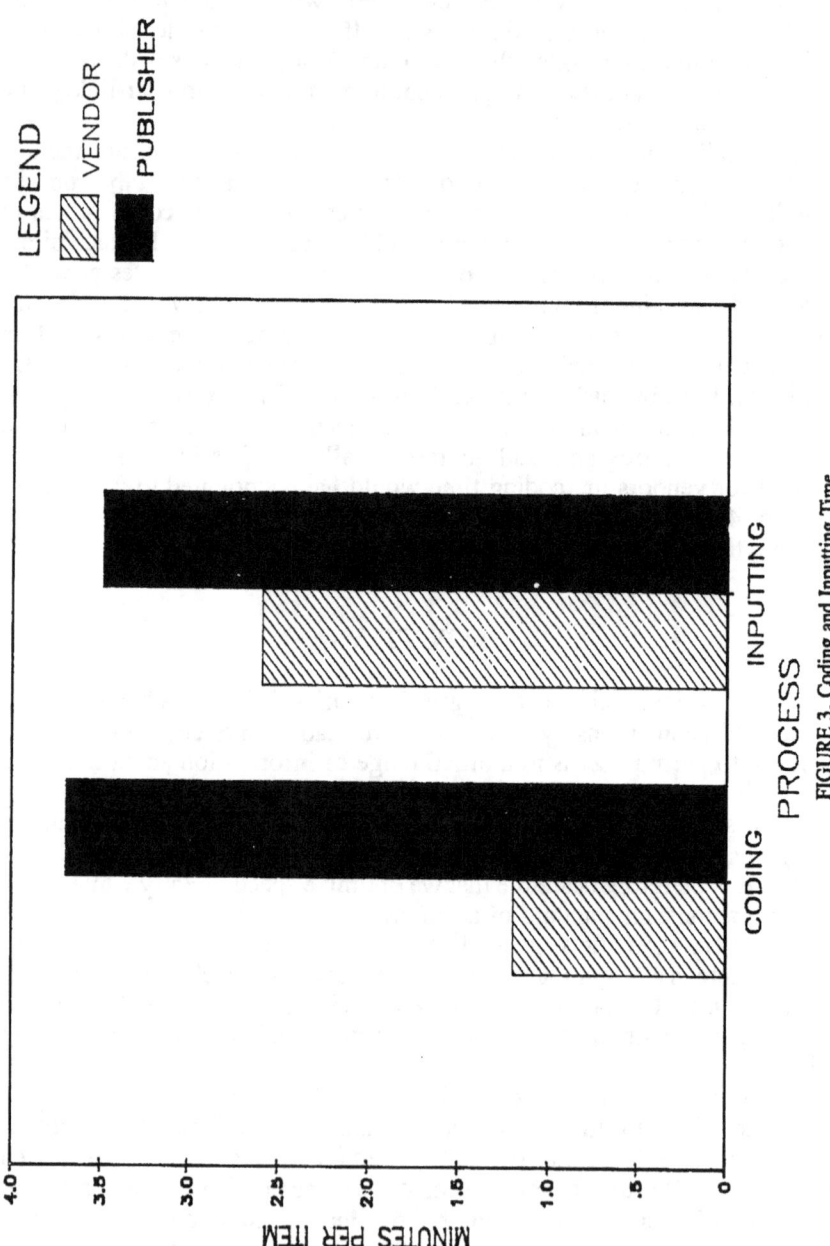

FIGURE 3. Coding and Inputting Time

at 2.6 minutes and orders needing the publisher address input with each order at 3.5 minutes. In our study sample the total inputting time for the vendor orders would have amounted to 6,149 minutes or 102.5 hours while the orders needing the publisher address would have required 8,277 minutes or 138 hours.

MAILING

We print orders on a daily basis. The automated system sorts orders internally by supplier and prints them. All individual forms are detached from the printout, batched by vendor or publisher, placed in an envelope, and forwarded to the mail room for posting. Typically, we will run between 100 and 200 order slips including both firm orders to vendors and direct orders to publishers. As shown in Figure 4, the unit time required to prepare the orders for mailing is clearly reduced as the number of orders for a single supplier increases. It takes 19 seconds to place one order in an envelope. If seven orders are stuffed in one envelope the average time per order is reduced to 7.8 seconds. The linear relationship is interrupted at eight slips because seven represents the maximum number of slips that can be held in a single envelope. This occurs again at 15 but not at 22 since larger manilla envelopes are used for batches of this size.

Once envelopes are stuffed, they must be sealed which again reinforces the economy of batched handling. The small white envelopes holding one to seven order slips take an average of 4.2 seconds to seal regardless of how many items they contain. The larger brown envelopes require some 15 seconds for sealing but they might hold as many as 30 or 40 slips so the unit time is considerably reduced.

Over and above the processing time discussed above, additional postage costs are incurred by sending out many individual slips as opposed to several batched orders. Single slips mailed to domestic vendors require postage in the amount of 22 cents, but batches of 25 or 30 slips can be mailed to a vendor for 56 cents. This economy is increased when it is considered that some vendors provide postage free mailing envelopes.

RECEIVING

Our acquisitions unit receives close to 300 books on a typical day. These arrive in all manner of packaging but the important consideration is the time required to unpack the incoming orders. Intermittent observation over a two week period revealed the following patterns in relation to receiving. Firm orders from vendors tended to come in the largest boxes,

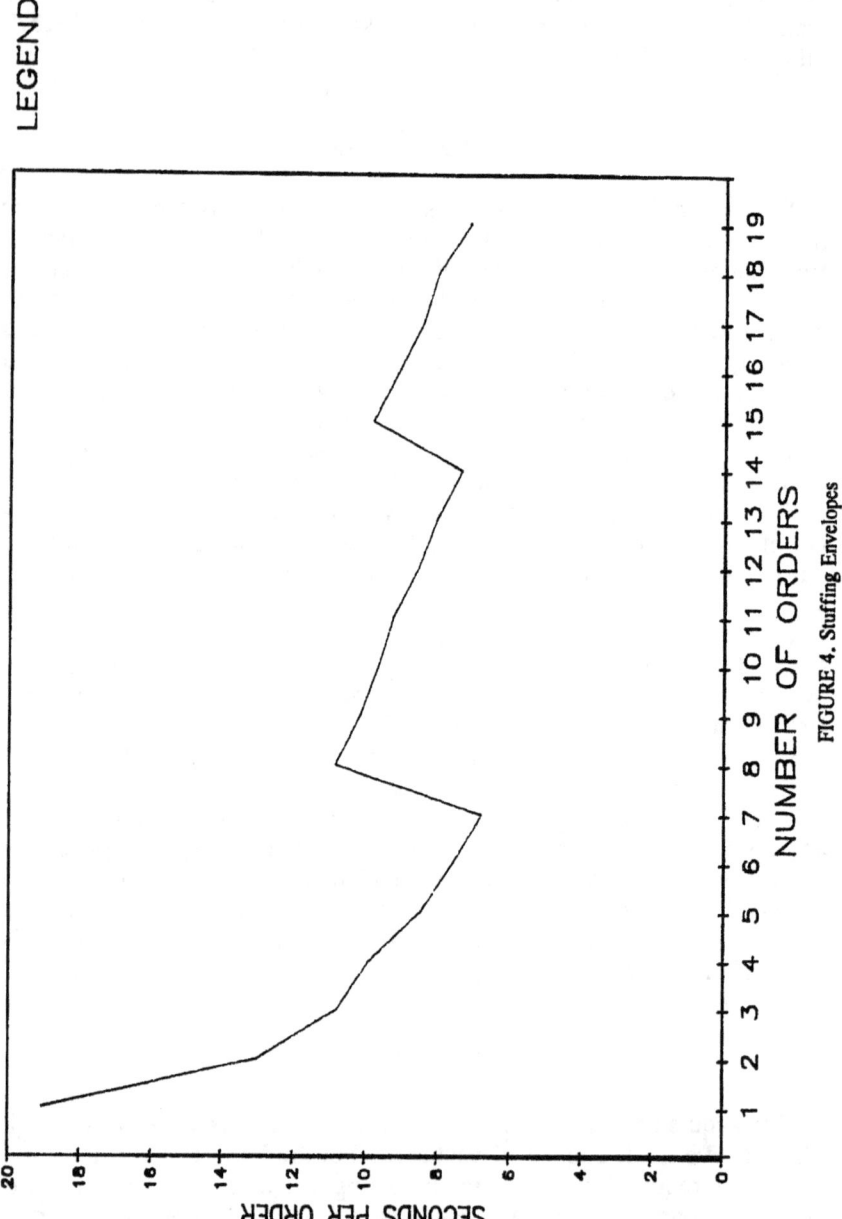

FIGURE 4. Stuffing Envelopes

averaging 26.5 pieces per box. This was followed by approval orders averaging 10.6 pieces per box and direct orders averaging 1.8 pieces each. Although large packages take longer to open and empty than do small packages, the time per piece is decidedly reduced as the number of pieces increases. Figure 5 illustrates that the average time for processing approval and firm orders is about 20 seconds whereas the per item time for publisher orders is 69 seconds.

These data include the physical opening of the box, removal of the books, checking off the books against the invoice or packing slip and marking the invoice as to the completeness of the shipment. Not included is the time required to check the automated system when orders arrive without a copy of our order as we request. This problem is relatively common when we order from a publisher and one which further adds to the costs of receiving direct orders. Our vendors rarely neglect to enclose a copy of our purchase order as they try to satisfy all our needs as a means of retaining our business.

PAYMENT

After materials have been received the corresponding verified invoices are forwarded to the bill payers for processing. The bill paying procedures include entering payment information in the automated acquisitions system, photocopying invoices, batching copies to be forwarded to the University central accounting office, and other related record-keeping activities. Studies were made comparing processing time for one invoice of 50 line items with 50 invoices with one line item each as illustrated in Figure 6. It was found in two separate observations, with two individual billpayers that it took 160 minutes and 175 minutes to process the 50 one-line item invoices. In marked contrast, the times recorded for the one 50-line invoices were 24 and 35 minutes respectively. These differences are primarily attributable to the following:

- the time required to process 50 separate invoices in the automated system (input invoice number and rate, verify the vendor name and address)
- the time required to photocopy 50 separate sheets
- the batching procedure which permits only a limited number of invoices to be attached to a single voucher
- the probability that the source of purchase will be doing enough business with the total University to require a unique code in the University system
- the time required to underline the payee and payee address

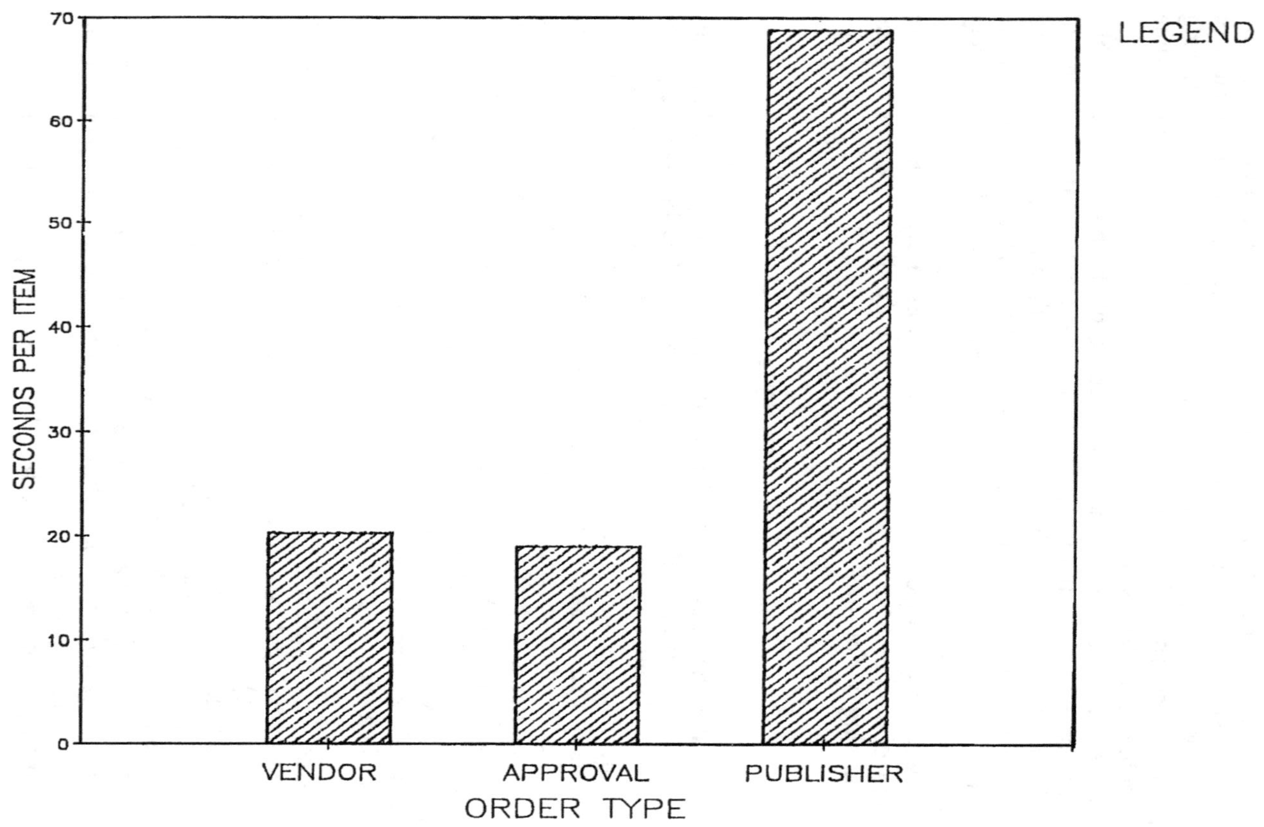

FIGURE 5. Box Opening

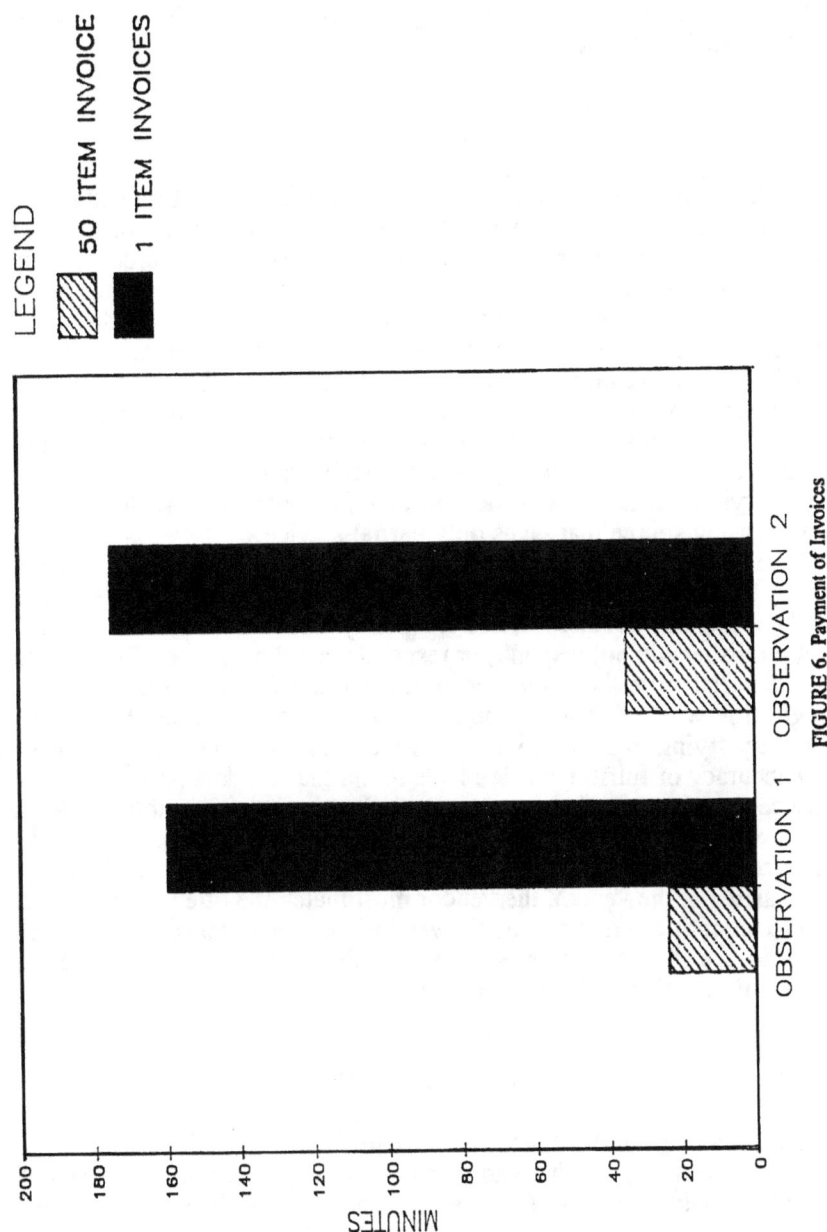

FIGURE 6. Payment of Invoices

The payment process is clearly and dramatically affected by the number of receipts from a specific source. The review of this process is enough to convince me that ordering directly from a publisher is a clear waste of staff time and energy.

THE CHOICE

As librarians, we are frequently reminded of studies of publisher and vendor performance as they relate to speed of fulfillment and rate of discount. Publishers sometimes promise large discounts for orders placed directly, but we, in practice, have found that their service is often slow, inaccurate and incomplete. Likewise, some vendors offer high discounts and thereby have committed themselves to supply only materials on which they receive large discounts from the publisher. Those vendors are performing a disservice to libraries because they can supply some materials at the high discount rate and the other materials will never be supplied. Vendors in this category need to receive a very clear message that their services are not only inadequate, but inappropriate. We do not need a purchasing source that gives only partial service.

Some vendors and publishers strive to conscientiously fill orders, but some of them fail miserably. Indeed, we sometimes wonder if the supplier really wants our business. More frequently than we would like we find that publishers do not respond, or respond very slowly, to our requests to buy material from them. We recognize that our order for one copy of a single title will result in a minimal profit for the publisher, but we are sincerely trying to acquire what we order and wish to do so with speed and accuracy of fulfillment. We have found that vendors perform a great service to us because they serve as a quality check on the publisher. Most of the vendors we use have only a minimal amount of stock. They must therefore order many of the titles we want from the publisher. When the titles arrive at the vendor, the vendor must match the title to our order. If an incorrect title is received by the vendor, the vendor takes the necessary steps to see that the order is properly filled. We, in turn, receive the correct title with no additional effort.

CONCLUSION

There can be and there are great variations: in the service performance from publisher to publisher and vendor to vendor. We can always switch vendors should the service not prove adequate, but we have no alternative should the publisher's service be inadequate. We are major clients to our vendors, but to at least some publishers we feel we are probably little more than a nuisance. We should encourage all publishers to sell to vendors so that our full needs can be filled by them. We would also hope that publishers would allow their publications to be offered on approval plans. The staff savings realized by going to vendors were vividly demonstrated by the study. If we were to use publishers instead of vendors, we would need more than twice the staff to perform the functions reviewed in the study. In no instance did we realize a staff savings by ordering from the publisher. Publishers sometimes require advanced payment and fulfilling this requirement, when large university processes are taken into account, can be lengthy and cumbersome.

By saving staff costs, we are also making a savings in other ways. Because we need less staff, we need less space to house the staff. Supplies and equipment needs are reduced proportionally. Our automated system costs are less because we have need for only a limited number of terminals for the staff. Because we are using vendors, the storage capacity of our system does not need space for hundreds of publisher addresses.

The source of purchase is a major factor in determining the actual cost of material added to a library. We have had our impressions reinforced by this study and strongly encourage publishers and vendors to work together with us so our patrons can be served in the most cost efficient manner.

Differential Pricing of Monographs and Serials

Christian M. Boissonnas

I would like to describe an event which happened recently at a midwestern university. The midwestern location is unimportant. It could have happened anywhere.

It is about 9:30 a.m., on a cold, dreary winter morning, the second day after the Christmas holiday. Outside a strong wind is whipping all that snow which nobody bothered to shovel after the holiday. Inside, it is the usual, soporific, 80 degrees. About one hour after the staff of the Serials Department of Battle Creek State University begins to open the mail, there are still four big book trucks of the stuff leftover from the holiday. The Chief Kardex Clerk, Joseph Heft, is checking in the latest issue of *Cambridge Quarterly* and struggling to stay awake. The invoice shows $45.00 as the subscription renewal price for this title. Dutifully, Heft pulls the pay record and starts writing $45.00 in the next available space. Through his fog, at the edge of his vision, he perceives a slip of paper tucked in behind the check-in card. Heft is a conscientious man. Sleepy though he is, he makes the supreme effort, reaches for the slip and opens it. Who knows, it may be a special routing instruction. But no, it is only the publisher's brochure advertising the new, low subscription price for *Cambridge Quarterly* of £20.00. If Heft has one fault, it is a weakness for numbers. He simply cannot leave them alone. "£20," he thinks to himself. "That's about $28 at the current rate of exchange. How much was that bill for? $45.00! Holy Rice Krispies! 60.71428% more! How can this be?"

Now fully awake, Heft reaches for the next serial to check in. It is the last issue of *Contemporary Review*. The back cover advertises the periodical for £15.50. The pay record, Heft discovers, shows that the subscription was just renewed for $50.00. "Wait a minute," Heft says to himself. "£15.50 is about $22. Maybe we renewed for more than one year." So he checks. But no, the renewal was for one year.

Deeply disturbed, Heft gathers his evidence and knocks on the door of the office of Jennifer Kellogg, Serials Librarian of Battle Creek State

---

Paper presented at the Conference on Pricing and Costs of Monographs and Serials, Oklahoma City, February 20-21, 1986.

© 1987 by The Haworth Press, Inc. All rights reserved.

University. Somnolent herself, Ms. Kellogg is idly thinking about the dinner which she will have at ALA in a few weeks with her good friend Kit Kennedy from Faxon. Rudely brought back to reality by the insistent knock on her door, she invites Heft to come in and listens to his tale of woe.

Kellogg is a devoted librarian. She works very hard at making sure all the work gets done, she conscientiously follows up on all problem serials, she goes to all the right meetings at ALA, and she tries to keep up with her professional literature. In the latter, however, she is not as successful, and upon her desk are, still unread, the last two years of *Serials Librarian* and three years of *Library Acquisitions: Practice and Theory*. It just so happens that, tucked in both journals, only inches away, are articles about British serials pricing.

Indeed, there are now a number of articles that explore the subject of discriminatory pricing in depth. In the last two years librarians have awakened to the existence of a problem and work is being done in a number of places to document it. Of particular importance to this paper is the work done in Missouri (two separate efforts: Hamaker and Astle[1] at the University of Missouri, and Ruschin[2] at Linda Hall, at the University of Michigan by Bob Houbeck,[3] and at the University of North Carolina by Marcia Tuttle.[4] Others are undoubtedly pursuing the topic but their findings have not yet appeared in the journals.

All writers tell a similar story, which I will paraphrase briefly from Tuttle's article on "North American Prices for British Scholarly Journals."

Until about 1976 British periodicals were available at two prices: one for the domestic market and one, somewhat higher, for the foreign market. Both were given in pound sterling. In 1976, a third price started appearing: one for the North American market stated in U.S. dollars. That price, in recent years, has increased more sharply than the other two prices, to the point now where the kinds of differentials which woke up our friend Heft are common: All papers from which I draw have plenty of examples. Hamaker and Astle studied 548 titles; I do not know how many Ruschin examined, but he cites data for 20, and Houbeck looked at 61.

It is tempting, but dangerous, to try to compare the titles from the various lists. Let me show you why with one example. The *Journal of Experimental Botany*, published by Oxford University Press, appears in both the Ruschin and the Hamaker and Astle studies. All agree that the U.K. domestic price is £95. One says that the North American price is $220, and the other, $222. Not a big difference, certainly one I can live with, although I have the uneasy feeling that there is a typo in one of them. But it could also be a difference in the accounting for shipping and handling charges. All agree that the rest-of-the-world price is £104. However Hamaker and Astle tell us that this translates to $146 ($220 minus

$74 which is the difference in dollars between the U.S. and overseas prices), while Ruschin tells us that it translates to $156. While I was willing to accept a $2 difference (1%), I am not willing to accept a $10 difference (7%) at face value. The problem, of course, is that they use different exchange rates.

You see the danger. We may be comparing apples and oranges. A further complication is that I do not know how the Missouri study factored in extra charges such as postage and handling. If they factored them in the same way, then the comparison between both sets of data is more meaningful than if they didn't.

But I am quibbling. Difficult though it may be to compare them, both studies make it abundantly clear that there is a serious problem which deserves our attention. I, who like Jennifer Kellogg was asleep at the wheel, thank them. I am now wide awake and catching up fast.

Let us look at a few of the data gathered by Michigan (see Table 1).

In Table 1 the rate for any title is obtained by dividing the U.S. price by the U.K. price. If we assume that the U.S. price is determined on the same basis as the U.K. price (i.e., not inflated), that number becomes the effective exchange rate. In other words, we see a pound sterling whose value fluctuates from $1.40 to the pound (for the *Anglo-Welsh Review*) to $3.23 (for the *Contemporary Review*). In fact, in 1985, the exchange rate fluctuated between ca. $1.08 and ca. $1.50. At no time did it go near $1.60, the lowest rate in Table 1.

Let us postulate that a reasonable markup for a foreign price over the

TABLE 1

British Periodicals: A Comparison of 1985 Prices, UK & USA

Title/Publisher	UK	USA	Rate*	% Diff, UK v. US
Anglo-Welsh Review (H.G. Walters)	£2.10	$2.10	$1.40	—
Cambridge Quarterly (Oxford Univ Pr)	£20.00	$45.00	$2.25	+61%
Contemporary Review	£15.50	$50.00	$3.23	+131%
Encounter	£18.00	$39.00	$2.17	+55%
German Life & Letters (B. Blackwell)	£32.00	$80.00	$2.50	+79%
Illustrated London News	£18.00	$23.00	$1.73	+24%
London Magazine	£12.50	$28.00	$2.24	+60%
London Review of Books	£17.20	$37.50	$2.17	+55%
Manchester Guardian Weekly	N.A.	$52.00	—	—
New Left Review	£25.00	$40.00	$1.60	+14%
Stand Magazine	£5.80	$12.50	$2.16	+54%
Times Literary Supplement	£40.00	$75.00	$1.88	+34%

*Exchange rate = Rate as of 6/84 & 9/85 (all prices above were taken from 1985 issues).
Source: see note 5.

domestic price is 30%. You may think that it should be less, 10-15%, but let us give the British publishers the benefit of the doubt and give them 30%. Looking at Table 1, it is hard to escape the conclusion that we are being taken to the cleaners.

Let us amend the Michigan table and convert all sterling prices to their U.S. equivalent, using an exchange rate somewhere between the official minimum and maximum for 1985. Let us use $1.30 (see Table 2).

My critics will immediately dismiss Table 2 on the ground that the percentages do not mean a thing because on any given day the exchange rate was not $1.30, but something else. They are, of course, right. These data cannot be used to say that such-and-such journal costs 92% more on the U.S. than the British market. But that is not why I computed them. What I was after first was to set all prices in the same currency. I get very confused when I try to compare dollars and pounds, especially when the exchange rate varies. Second, I wanted to remove the effect of currency fluctuations to see how the data looked, especially since Table 1 did not give me real rates. The $1.30 rate is correct +/− 15%, which is close enough for what I am trying to demonstrate.

If you increase the exchange rate used in Table 2 by 15%, that is, assuming the worst bias in which all numbers favor the U.S. buyers at the expense of the U.K. publishers, there is still a major problem. Let us assume this bias and adjust Table 2 accordingly. This is the same as saying that during 1985 the exchange rate was not $1.30 but $1.50, or the highest that it was all year. The new numbers appear in Table 3.

TABLE 2

British Periodicals: A Comparison of 1985 Prices, UK & USA
Assuming an Exchange Rate of $1.30 for £1.00

Title/Publisher	UK	USA	% Diff, UK v. US
Anglo-Welsh Review (H.G. Walters)	$2.73	$2.73	0
Cambridge Quarterly (Oxford Univ Pr)	$26.00	$45.00	+73%
Contemporary Review	$20.15	$50.00	+148%
Encounter	$23.40	$39.00	+66%
German Life & Letters (B. Blackwell)	$41.60	$80.00	+92%
Illustrated London News	$23.40	$23.40	0
London Magazine	$16.25	$28.00	+72%
London Review of Books	$22.36	$37.50	+67%
Manchester Guardian Weekly	N.A.	$52.00	—
New Left Review	$32.50	$40.00	+23%
Stand Magazine	$7.54	$12.50	+66%
Times Literary Supplement	$52.00	$75.00	+44%

TABLE 3

British Periodicals: A Comparison of 1985 Prices, UK & USA
Assuming an Exchange Rate of $1.50 for £1.00

Title/Publisher	UK	USA	% Diff, UK v. US
Anglo-Welsh Review (H.G. Walters)	$3.15	$3.15	0
Cambridge Quarterly (Oxford Univ Pr)	$30.00	$45.00	+50%
Contemporary Review	$23.25	$50.00	+115%
Encounter	$27.00	$39.00	+44%
German Life & Letters (B. Blackwell)	$48.00	$80.00	+66%
Illustrated London News	$27.00	$27.00	0
London Magazine	$18.75	$28.00	+49%
London Review of Books	$25.80	$37.50	+45%
Manchester Guardian Weekly	N.A.	$52.00	—
New Left Review	$37.50	$40.00	+6%
Stand Magazine	$8.70	$12.50	+43%
Times Literary Supplement	$60.00	$75.00	+25%

What have we accomplished by giving our British friends a better exchange rate than they actually got? We got the *New Left Review* and *Times Literary Supplement* within the 30% that we assumed above to be a fair markup over the domestic price. That's all. In other words, we are still being taken to the cleaners.

The thing that bothers me about the Michigan data is that they do not deal with what I see as the worst part of the problem. For reasons which you will see later, I am quite willing to grant them a 50% or higher markup on their foreign sales. What really rankles, however, is that third price, the North American price I mentioned when paraphrasing Marcia Tuttle's article. The fact that it is generally higher than the other foreign price is, of course, not accidental. To understand how obnoxious that price really is, let us look at an extract from Table 1 of the Hamaker and Astle study (see Table 4).

The average difference between the U.S. and U.K. prices for the above titles is $88.52. The average difference between the U.S. and overseas price is $74.14. In other words, we pay $89 a title more for this sample of titles than U.K. libraries do. As I said above, this does not necessarily disturb me. But we pay $74 more per title than other, non-U.K. libraries in the world. That bothers me. In fact it bothers me so much that I find it very difficult to open my mind and calmly accept the perfectly rational explanations of the British publishing industry.

These, again paraphrasing Tuttle, go something like this:

The major problem leading to the North American price was the sharp

TABLE 4

Subscription Prices of Selected British Journals

Title/Publisher	UK Price	Overseas Price	U.S. Price	Difference in $ between US & UK	Difference in $ between US & overseas price
Animal Behavior					
Balliere Tindall	£57	£70	$155.00	$75.06(+)	$56.83(+)
Annals of Human Bio.					
Taylor & Francis	£59	£59	$185.00	$102.00(+)	$102.00(+)
Brain					
Oxford Univ. Press	£34	£38.5	$80.00	$32.32(+)	$26.00(+)
Brit. J. Haematology					
BlackwellSci.	£73.5	£80	$187.50	$84.42(+)	$73.50(+)
Brit. J. Nutrition					
Cambridge U.P.	£104	–	$270.00	$124.14(+)	–
Cambridge Law J.					
Cambridge U.P.	£16	–	$45.00	$22.56(+)	–
Clinical Physiology					
Blackwell Sci.	£75	£90	$180.00	$74.81(+)	$53.78(+)
Erodic Theory & Dynamical System					
Cambridge U.P.	£65	–	$180.00	$88.84(+)	
Egronomics [sic]					
Taylor & Francis	£84	£84	$259.00	$141.19(+)	$141.19(+)
Ergonomics Abstracts					
Taylor & Francis	£80	£80	$252.00	$139.89(+)	$139.80(+)

Source: see note 6.

fall of the dollar in the mid 1970s. Because periodical prices are set nine months before the year in which they are due to appear, the need for British publishers to cover themselves against a less valuable dollar was paramount. In addition, it costs a lot more to do business in the U.S. than elsewhere. Since so many of their subscribers are in the U.S., they get the journals faster if they are produced there. Printing and distribution costs in the U.S. being what they are, it is evident, or should be to any well-intentioned person, that foreign publishers must charge more here to make the same profit.

I can accept that argument. Most of it anyway. I may quibble about whether these costs really are 50% or more higher than in the U.K., but the argument is basically sound. What troubles me, however, is what happened next. The dollar did not stay down forever. In fact, it recovered very handsomely in the early 80s while the pound took a nosedive. Prices continued their upward climb. Why? Because, in Tuttle's words, they "now depend heavily on the income these North American subscriptions bring [them]."[7] In other words, having gotten used to this nice additional income in the 70s, and having to protect themselves against a deteriorating market at home, they could not bear to give it up. That's what I am having trouble accepting. That, and the fact that we let them. Yes, we did. For 8 years. This is how long it took the more alert among us to wake up. Jennifer Kellogg at Battle Creek State was no worse than the rest of us. We might not have been dreaming about dinner with Kit Kennedy, but we were asleep all the same. But let me return to this point later. First let us finish the review of the problem.

One of the points which the British make is that they are no worse to us than we are to them. We, too, charge them a price for our publications which is substantially higher than our domestic price. Let us see how true that is.

The *Newsletter* of the American Studies Library Group, a British organization, includes a number of items in its 1979 and 1980 issues dealing with University Microfilms' pricing policy in the U.K. The charge against UMI was that, by manipulating handling costs, the exchange rate, and a 15% surcharge on business done in the U.K., it was marking up its publications 30%.[8] UMI, naturally, denied the charge. I am not going to go into a deep analysis here about who is right. By simply applying whatever reason I have left after 21 years in this business, I will say that 30% seems a bit high. If I were on the receiving end I would certainly want it justified to me. On the other side, the British case does not seem all that clear cut. Shipping and handling at 13% for a photocopy of a thesis is on the high side, but I have paid a lot higher.

Let us just say that there is enough in this dispute to suggest that there may be a problem for U.K. libraries similar to the one we have and see what else there may be.

There are data which strongly suggest that some of our monograph publishers are also feathering their nests, some more than others. The following table is copied from the September 1979 *Newsletter* of the American Studies Library Group (see Table 5).

According to these data the average markup is 44%. These numbers were compiled by Tom Slatner, a book dealer, using "books supplied by him in February and March 1979 at a conversion rate of $2.07 to the pound."[10]

So our publishers jack up their prices to sell abroad, or at least did so in 1979. Undoubtedly their shipping and distribution costs are higher, and why should U.S. consumers subsidize British book buyers. Right? Without having any data to back me up, I would say that 30% or so ought to cover that. After all, we allowed that earlier to U.K. publishers. Obviously 30% is adequate for Freeman, Plenum, and Houghton Mifflin because, if there is one thing of which I am absolutely convinced, it is that they do not sell books in the U.K. at a loss. So, what are those 51%, 66%, and 76% markups?

TABLE 5
U.S. Publishers' Sterling Price

Publisher	Markup	Publisher	Markup
Academic	36	Kennikat	76
Addison	56	McGraw	43
Allyn & Bacon	51	Macmillan	46
Arizona	27	Michigan	34
California	36	MIT	45
Chicago	49	Nebraska	61
Columbia	33	Penn. State	45
Freeman	31	Plenum	31
Greenwood	44	Prentice Hall	48
Harper	47	Princeton	42
Harvard	48	Rand McNally	38
Heath	35	Scarecrow	38
Houghton	32	Toronto	38
Illinois	66	Van Nostrand	68
Indiana	46	Wiley	42
Johns Hopkins	40	Wisconsin	45
Kelley	42	Yale	46

Source: see note 9.

To their credit, the ASLG people were not completely satisfied with the Slatner data. They felt that the sample might have been too small, and that some prices might have been out-of-date, or plain wrong.[11] So they got some copies of orders from Slatner for books from five U.S. university presses, checked them out, and did a survey which resulted in the following table (see Table 6).

Seeing this sort of study, one can contend until doomsday that because the sample is small, or the number of order for each press is small, or not all appropriate statistical tests were done, the study is fatally flawed. This is usually what the people on the short end of the stick say when they bother to say anything at all. This may be true. However my purpose here was not to prove that American publishers discriminate against U.K. or other foreign libraries, but to explore the likelihood that they do. This, I think, I have done. Let us apply the Law of Reason, plus the Law of Spontaneous Combustion (where there's smoke there's fire). It seems safe to say that some U.S. publishers among those in Tables 5 and 6 above are using objectionable "revenue enhancing" procedures. In other words, the British are right, we do it to them too. Some, mostly publishers, may disagree on the facts, but it is a perfectly valid hypothesis to prove or disprove with a large-scale formal study. There is little doubt in my mind that the results of such a study would confirm the data which I have seen.

Before you accuse me of being on the side of the bad guys, let us remember two essential differences between their situation and ours. The first is that, bad though our publishers with their markups may be, they seem to discriminate equally among all foreigners. I have yet to see a report of a pricing scheme equivalent to that North American price. Please note that I used the word "yet." The second difference has to do with the truly objectionable British practice of compelling book vendors and subscription agents to reveal their customers' identity. This, of course, is to protect their artificially high North American price. Again, I do not know of any U.S. publisher that does that.

The Missouri group and Marcia Tuttle did us a big favor by bringing this problem to the surface. In a previous conference where I heard this topic discussed I observed people expressing more or less vehemently their anger at their treatment by these U.K. publishers. All I ask, before we give vent to our rightful indignation, is that we look objectively at the whole situation, not just half of it. I have yet to hear anyone in this country condemn a U.S. publisher for its 60% markup of titles that it sells in the U.K.

So far I have discussed the issue of price discrimination on both sides of the Atlantic. Our attitude toward each other, two allies who are probably as close as allies can get, is ironic. Given this state of affairs you should not be surprised when I tell you that we, Americans, do it to ourselves as well.

In a study of price discrimination by academic journals in the fields of economics and business, Edward Dyl found the following (see Table 7).

Unfortunately Dyl also included in his sample the major European journals. We have only his word that "there is no reason to believe that this casual approach to sample selection imparts any bias to the study."[14] I would have preferred a sample of U.S. journals only. Nevertheless, until

TABLE 6

AUPG £ Prices as % of US $ List Prices

Publisher	Slatner's original figures at $2.07:£ (rate Feb/Mar 1979)	Rechecked at $2.07:£1	ASLG Survey at $2.07:£1	ASLG Survey at $2.16:£1
Illinois	166%	145%	152%[1]	—
Indiana	146%	145%	139%[2]	—
Nebraska	161%	145%	145%[3]	—
Penn State	145%	144%	147%[4]	—
Wisconsin	145%	144%	146%[5]	—
Average	153%	145%	146%	148%

[1]Fall/Winter 1977/78 Catalogue. [2]Spring/Summer and Winter/Fall Catalogue 1978. [3]Fall/Winter 1977/78 Catalogue. [4]Spring/Summer 1978 Catalogue. [5]Spring 1978 Catalogue. (£ prices from BBIP or BNB)

Source: See note 12.

TABLE 7
Pricing Policies of Academic Journals

Type of publisher	Mean individual price (US$)	Mean library price (US$)	Library price as % of indiv. price	% that discriminate
Total sample (N = 76)	18.42 (.96)	27.35 (2.05)	148	59
Profess. Assns. (N = 30)	21.48 (1.56)	26.98 (2.68)	126	47
University (N = 26)	12.04 (.81)	16.35 (1.47)	136	58
Private pub. (N = 20)	22.13 (1.73)	42.19 (4.81)	191	80

Note: N = number of observations. Figures in parentheses are standard deviations.
Source: See note 13.

proven otherwise, I am willing to start with the assumption that his statement is correct.

That this discrimination exists is something that most, if not all, have known for a long time. I am willing to bet, however, that not many of you have thought of it when you think about the British problem. And yet, in order to deal successfully with price discrimination, I think that you must because they are different facets of the same problem.

We, as librarians, are not used to thinking about our profession as a business. And yet, especially in the book buying field, we deal with business all the time. What is happening both in the U.K. and here is that the publishers are simply responding to market forces. We have not done much up to now to influence, let alone direct, those forces. I recommend to you the Dyl article, the source of Table 7, which explains the economic and legal theories behind what is happening in terms simple enough for me to understand. He writes about the publishers of journals as monopolists who are practicing price discrimination. This discrimination may, in fact, be illegal in this country but he stops short of making the accusation, suggesting only that this facet of the problem should be studied further.

My point is that the British and American publishers behave in substantially the same way. They set up different price structures because they find it advantageous to do so and we let them. At least we have let them up to now.

Before you wring your hands in utter frustration about what to do, think for a minute about what already has been done, at least as far as the British problem is concerned. The alarm raised by our Missouri colleagues has resulted in much discussion and some action. ALA has studied the problem and determined so far that there was not much that it could do except negotiate. Marcia Tuttle reports in her paper that some publishers have recognized their guilt and intend to make amends, but that it will take some time.[15] At least one publisher (Taylor and Francis) has reportedly frozen their U.S. prices as a first step.

What this suggests to me is that the battle is far from being lost. A problem existed, some people raised their voices about it, were heard, and some change occurred. We do have some power in the market place, if we choose to exercise it. But before we congratulate ourselves about having conquered the British menace and go on to other things, let us pause for a minute.

For one thing, we have not conquered the British problem. We never will completely because there will always be a publisher who will refuse to go along with the majority knowing full well that we will keep buying from him anyway. The most we will ever see is the situation controlled enough so that we do not feel exploited.

For another thing, our vigilance must be constant. Market forces are always at work, whether or not we choose to recognize them. We need to respond much more rapidly than we have in this case to changes in the overall equation. We cannot allow ourselves to assume that, when the next crisis comes along, the Missouri folks will be there to alert us. We all share a responsibility to raise the alarm.

Unfortunately Jennifer Kellogg could not be here today. She spent her whole travel budget for the year at ALA last month. Nevertheless she met with enough people who shared her concern that her consciousness was raised. She communicated to Josef Heft the importance of being particularly alert to discrepancies between invoice price and prices on publishers' announcements or issues.

On January 25, 1986, he saw a letter from Knut Dorn of Harrassowitz, and read it. His pulse quickened. He had just noted that VCH Publishers in Weinheim, West Germany, had advised Harrassowitz of a major policy change: they would no longer sell their journals to Harrassowitz "at the European list price for [their] customers in North America."[16] Later on Dorn added: "Beginning with 1986, they [VCH] are forcing us to buy the journal needed for our North American customers from their U.S. outlet in Deerfield Beach, Florida, at the dramatically higher U.S. dollar prices."[17]

Ten minutes later, his composure regained but hands still trembling, Heft knocked on Kellogg's door.

NOTES

1. Charles Hamaker and Deana Astle, "Recent Pricing Patterns in British Journal Publishing." *Library Acquisitions: Practice and Theory*, 8 (1984):225-232.

2. Siegfried Ruschin, "Why Are Foreign Subscription Rates Higher for American Libraries Than They Are for Subscribers Elsewhere?" *Serials Librarian*, 9(3) (1985):7-17.

3. Robert L. Houbeck, "British Periodical Pricing." (Unpublished study conducted at the University of Michigan, November 1985).
4. Marcia Tuttle, "North American Prices for British Scholarly Journals." (Paper delivered at the Conference on Issues in Book and Serials Acquisitions: All You Never Wanted to Know about Finances, College of Charleston, Charleston, SC, November 7-8, 1985).
5. Houbeck, "British Periodical Pricing," p. 5.
6. Hamaker and Astle, "Pricing Patterns," p. 227.
7. Tuttle, "North American Prices," p. 8.
8. American Studies Library Group, *Newsletter* (April 1979):21-24, and (February 1980): 14-15.
9. Ibid. (September 1979):28-29.
10. Ibid., p. 28.
11. Ibid. (February 1980):17.
12. Ibid., p. 18.
13. Edward A. Dyl, "A Note on Price Discrimination by Academic Journals." *Library Quarterly*, 53(2) (1983):164.
14. Ibid., p. 162.
15. Tuttle, "North American Prices," p. 13.
16. Knut Dorn, letter to Elaine Walker, Head, Serials Department, Cornell University Library, January 15, 1986.
17. Ibid.

The Cost of Global Serials: The Vendor's Perspective

Kit Kennedy

I recall in 1982 when visiting a major university library in the Midwest. I was talking with the head of technical services about foreign serials. Our conversation came around to the definition, as it frequently does, of serials. What exactly does your library consider a serial? He responded that his department viewed serials by the standard library school definition. But the twinkle in his eye suggested that I should pause before responding, for a probable punch line was on its way. He pithily summed it up when he quipped that serials are those things that have the greatest probability of going awry, in the most parts, with the greatest frequency. As is often the case, humor, grounded in frustrating reality, has its validity.[1]

Seriously, there are numerous studies which aptly chart, diagnose, and passionately bemoan this inherent characteristic of serials. What is germane to our discussion is that this temperament of serials contributes to escalating cost. Before we examine this in greater detail, let me review the parameters of this paper and a few underlying assumptions. This paper explores the cost of global serials from the vendor's perspective and offers a framework for the cooperative interaction among users (libraries), suppliers (vendors), and sources (publishers) of information.

COMMON VOCABULARY: STANDARDIZATION

A noted philosopher argues that when we think, we think in a language. I liberally broaden this definition and suggest that while we think in a language, it is linguistic overlap, or the articulation of a commonly accepted and understood vocabulary, which allows us to communicate, to understand each other.

It is commonly agreed that we live in an information society. We are in fact bombarded by data; at times overwhelmed at the technology that permits us to create, store, retrieve, manipulate, sell, and license information. Yet, at present we lack a comprehensive vocabulary that allows us to communicate adequately about this phenomenon. Libraries, vendors, and publishers are not exempt; we are often in the center of this predicament.

In tandem with the need for a common language is the development and acceptance of standardized code for automated identification of information. The work of two organizations is noted. Programs are underway by SISAC (Serials Industry Systems Advisory Committee); tests with libraries, several scientific and technical publishers, as well as system vendors are scheduled for April-September 1986. These tests will measure the success of a standardized bar code, in machine-readable form that identifies a serial issue to the article level.[2]

More than 37 years SISAC's senior, NISO, National Information Standards Organization, focuses its campaigns to develop standards for those involved in handling information—libraries, vendors, publishers, information specialists. Two of the most recognized NISO programs are ISSN and ISBN. NISO participates in the international standards organization, ISO (International Organization of Standardization) which seeks to initiate standards on the global scale.

A common vocabulary and standards for automated transmittal of information are insufficient without mutual cooperation and compatibility.

THE COOPERATIVE FRAMEWORK: USERS, SUPPLIERS, SOURCES

In the past, the subscription vendor's role consisted of supplying a library with a journal, paying the publisher, invoicing the library for the issues and any additional issues; claiming upon request of the client, and providing rudimentary reports, usually on the status of claims. But the proliferation of information as well as the increase in the number and specialization of publishers dramatically change the role of the vendor. Libraries demand complex and sophisticated services from their vendors, often customized management reports for budgetary forecasting. Technology is applied to automate the previously manual functions of the library, especially the acquisitions tasks including serials. The benefits of this automation are efficient, cost-effective ways to process information. Online networks emerge which now link library with vendor with publisher on a global scale.

In broader terms the library, in our model, becomes the user; the vendor becomes the supplier; and the publishers emerge as the source.[3] This triangle communicating by online connections results in increased speed and accuracy of ordering and claiming with ultimate reduction in the cost of supplying information. One highly automated vendor sees its mission as working with both the users (library) and the sources.[4]

Electronic mail is frequently a means of users (libraries) and suppliers (vendors) to communicate, as well, of course, users (library) to users (library). This communication usually takes the form of electronic message switching, online ordering and claiming. But vendors are seeking opportunities to work creatively and cost effectively with publishers. Recent developments electronically link suppliers (vendors) with sources (publishers). One example of a functioning system which electronically hooks supplier with sources (publishers) allows these sources (publishers) to update their rate and publishing status information, and pull off orders and claims.[5]

At the crux of this interplay between users-supplier-sources is the ability of the supplier (vendor) to maintain and, more importantly, to update a comprehensive title file database from the sources of information (publishers). The responsiveness to change and ease of access to an international title file are critical.

One note of caution, in our model we defined the source generally as the traditional publisher; however, the PC revolution challenges our definition of a publisher. Improvements in hardware coupled with rapidly decreasing costs of extra storage, indicate that the personal computer will be the powerful workstation in the next five years.[6] Electronic networks will link authors working at home with readers and provide document delivery to users accessing that network. Consider the impact on research and scholarly publishing in particular. Information is online, instantaneous, and highly accessible to those who enter the information channels. The danger is that information will be available only to those who own, rent, or, more significantly, control the information channels.

GLOBAL SERIALS

Within this context of our users-suppliers-sources framework, let us return to a definition of serial. Pragmatically, in this information age, a serial is first and foremost information; information which is produced in parts (by sources), disseminated in parts (by suppliers), and received in parts (by users). At present, its primary format is print; however, we witness increasing successes and forays of serials produced in other media — electronic publishing, document delivery, and optical disk technology to name a few.

From the vendor's perspective, a fundamental and obvious aspect of the cost of serials is its price (the money which the publisher demands). A quick look through the 1986 edition of *The Almanac* points out that our task to determine the price of global serials is herculean if not impossible. According to *The Almanac*,[7] there are 11 major world groups: North America, South America, Central America, Caribbean Region, Europe, Middle East, Far East, Southeast Asia, Oceania, and Africa. In turn, these eleven groups reflect a total of 162 countries. A closer perusal of these individual nations shows that the majority of these 162 diverse countries have their own currency and speak different languages. The variables increase when you realize that many of these countries recognize multiple languages.

In theory it is possible that every country publishes at least one serial in its officially recognized languages. Suppose all publishers were part of a well-organized trade and could provide reliable publishing data. At the least, it would still take a supercharged spreadsheet to handle numerous calculations.

What then do we realistically need to know to predict the price of global serials? We need to foresee shifts in world economy and world politics of these 162 nations; predict the market shifts in interest and influence in the sciences and technology; predict the acquisitions and mergers of corporations, including the publishing community; and predict the impact of emerging forms of dissemination of information, especially electronic formats. Impossible?

Of course, the above scenario dramatizes the difficulties in absolutely predicting global serial prices. We can, however, judge prices by reviewing pricing trends as recorded in the recognized price studies.[8] These studies are based on prices in vendors' title file databases. Once again we see the significance in the vendors' comprehensive database in managing serial pricing.

PLACE OF PUBLICATION

The place of publication plays an increasing role both in the definition and cost of global serials. The phrase "country of origin" is well known and designates a library's practice for ordering serials from a vendor domiciled in the particular country from which the serial is published. The rationale is a country-of-origin vendor has language expertise and strong ties to its national publishing community. That vendor can supply trade as well as the more scholarly and esoteric titles. It is not my point to argue either in favor or against this practice. However, publication locations have changed, increasing dramatically in the past two decades. It is common for serials to list two or three places of publication — one inevitably a U.S. city. Responding to growth markets, European publishers (especially scientific and technical publishers) opened fully staffed and automated U.S. offices to handle sales and marketing as well as editorial functions. Elsevier in New York City; Pergamon in Elmsford, NY; the Kluwer companies in Hinoham, MA; Blackwell in Boston, MA; Birkhauser in Cambridge, MA; VCH (formerly Verlag Chemie) in Deerfield Beach, FL, are examples of this burgeoning phenomena. This migration of publishers opening offices in the U.S. has three major ramifications. It challenges the definition of country-of-origin as a national birthright. Second, international publishing — highly automated and market-sensitive in a competitive arena — emerges. Geographic boundaries quickly fade. The publishing output of serials is reflected in the international vendor's title file. Third, this competitive publishing market with its high costs of production and selling costs, pressures serials to recoup their initial start-up costs (developmental and test-marketing). One highly respected international publisher indicated in a conversation that the guideline for journal survival in their shop is three years. After the initial launch, a journal has three years to make itself financially solvent and contributing positively to that publisher's bottom line. Of course, this publisher cautioned that for reasons of prestige, preeminence in the market, or corporate politics there are those select journals allowed to squeeze past that three year dictum. While three years might seem arbitrary, publishers, like libraries and vendors, are in the information business.

Publishing Output

Libraries are painfully aware of the rapid escalation in price of serials. Added pressure is put on library budgets since serials have proliferated at an outstanding increase in the last 20 years. Once again international vendors are accurate sources to reflect the percentage of change in serials publication activity. One such vendor's database shows an overall increase in the number of serials in the decade 1974-1985 to be a staggering 174.1%.[9] This is based on the increase in the vendor's database. These serials include both active and inactive serials. Active titles include prepaid subscriptions and "bill later" titles. Inactive refer to temporary suspended/status in question, additional information required, order directs, previous, variant, split, merged; and discontinued.

Why is there a staggering increase in the number of serials? Automation and technology place greater emphasis on specialization; publishers produce serials often for a highly focused and immediate (information hungry) audience. This specialization causes publishers to be conservative in their print runs. Smaller print runs affect libraries in three distinct ways: serial prices tend to be higher because the unit cost is expensive. A smaller print places greater importance on timely ordering of new titles. Finally, and critical to the academic library, small print runs place added importance in claiming for nonreceipt or damaged copies and play havoc with a library's program of filling in incomplete runs of serials.

Foreign Exchange Rate

No discussion of cost is complete without mentioning the foreign exchange rate. Remember in our scenario on the factors which determine global serial prices, we raised the need to foresee changes in world politics and economy. It is after all, world politics and economy which greatly determine the foreign exchange rate. Let us consider the five principle "foreign" publishing countries: The Netherlands, Germany, the U.K., France, and Switzerland. For the library in North America, it is obvious that the strength and decline of the U.S. dollar either means more buying or less purchasing power. With a strong U.S. dollar, U.S. libraries can afford "foreign" serials; a weak U.S. dollar portends higher costs and less buying power for "foreign" serials. A review of the average price of the foreign titles for 1976 through 1984,[10] concludes with the following:

1977-1980	68% increase
1977-1982	86.8% increase
1982-1984	3.9% decrease (strong dollar)
1976-1984	82.9% overall increase

Average prices for "foreign" serial titles[11] are listed below (prices given in U.S. dollars):

1976	42.00
1977	43.00
1978	47.00
1979	56.00
1980	71.00
1981	78.00
1982	80.00
1983	78.00
1984	76.00

The above illustrates the delicate balance of world economy and the foreign exchange.

Dual Pricing

What other factors affect pricing? Dual pricing issues,[12] especially with British publishers, is a hotly contested and ALA monitored topic. Other have researched and suggested courses of action. It appears for the present that British publishers agreed to maintain a consistent pricing schedule based on the final destination of the serial.

THE VENDOR'S PERSPECTIVE ON SERIAL COSTS

So far, in our discussion of cost of international serials, we explored the intricacies of price or what the vendor must pay for a global serial. On the topic of price we took a closer look at place of publication, the print run, degree of publishing specialization, and the exchange rate.

In additional to price, the complexity and array of services offered; hiring and ongoing training of personnel; degree of inhouse automation;

commitment to long-term research and development to efficiently apply technology to practical, client-driven, problem-solving programs should be concerns and goals of any major serial vendor. These should be executed within the parameters of providing excellent services and within the context of cost containment.

Claiming

No discussion on the vendor's perspective on cost would be complete without a review of claiming. A study[13] conducted at the University of North Carolina canvassing the university members of the Association of Research Libraries (ARL) concludes that claiming ranks third in importance of vendor service and performance by these libraries. Other pertinent findings of this study include frequency of use of major domestic and foreign serial agents and the percentage of total orders. (The data were not divided by international serials agent.)

Both library and vendor work toward efficient procedures to produce, record, and, most importantly, to resolve claims. Automated serial check-in software packages and systems, whether vendor-supplied or library-developed, should provide efficient ways to handle claims and assist in reducing costs With a well-designed system, libraries have more control of their claiming with greater positive results.

Vendors deal with the publishers or the publishers' designated handlers such as a fulfillment house. Online connects between libraries, vendors, and the growing online network of vendors and publishers increase the efficiency of claiming. Marcia Tuttle's recent, excellent and balanced study on fulfillment centers provides an indepth and practical view of these companies. Her article defines fulfillment houses, reviews the type of problems incurred and suggests ways libraries and vendors can work together for improved results. The following striking statistic clearly sums up the library's relationship with the fulfillment center:

> One fulfillment center does only 2% and another only 1.5% of its business with libraries, but I am told that 50% of their complaints come from library subscriptions.[14]

Additional information from a vendor's database indicates that as of January 1986 six major fulfillment centers handled 206 popular titles. They are as follows:

Fulfillment Center	No. of titles
Neodata Services, Inc.	96
Times Mirror Magazine, Inc.	4

Fulfillment Center	No. of titles
Palm Coast and Data Ltd.	5
Fulfillment Corporation of America	9
Meredith Corporation	21
Communications Data Services	71
TOTAL	206[15]

While the 99% perfect answer to fulfillment centers might not come for years, however, it is this spirit of working together that will help discover a working solution for all of us.

CONCLUSIONS

Clearly, there is no magic formula to predict the price of global serials. However, this paper does point out that reliable forecasting tools are at a library's disposal in the form of recognized price studies. We have seen the creative, problem-solving power that is inherent in the vendor's on-line title file database and the creative ways those databases can be put to cooperative use with vendors and publisher. We return to our initial model of users, sources, and suppliers. The fluidity of technology and the costs involved point toward fostering a partnership attitude among the users, sources, and suppliers.

If we cannot absolutely predict and be involved, we can cooperate to manage these costs.

NOTES

1. Norman D. Stevens provides tongue-in-check definition of serials. "An obsolete term for a publication format in which a large number of information content pieces (incops) were packaged together with a generic title. . . . Serials as such went out of existence by 2009." See Norman D. Stevens, "Selections from a Dictionary of Libinfosci Terms," *Technical Services Quarterly*, 1, no. 1/2 (Fall/Winter 1983):259-260.

2. Ted Goessling and Mary Ellen Clapper, "Bar Codes and Serial Publications," *Editing History*, 6-10.

3. The framework for this user-supplier-source model is derived from a speech by Richard R. Rowe, President and CEO of The Faxon Company, delivered at the 4th Annual Linx Users Meeting in Boston, MA, on November 14, 1984.

4. Vendors such as The Faxon Company, Westwood, MA. See note 5.

5. An example of one functioning system which electronically connects vendors with publishers is PubLinx, Faxon's international service linking publisher with Faxon. Publishers on PubLinx have access to their own titles and title rates files on Faxon's title file database. These publishers receive claim notices and cancellation requests, customer address change notifications and back issue orders online. Publishers respond online to claims by entering their comments into the online claim file.

Publishers have access to the electronic message switching file, Linx Courier, and can communicate electronically with Faxon on customer service requests, notification of changes in rates, or on Infoserv to add and update their own advertising screens. At present this growing PubLinx network includes John Wiley and Sons, Johns Hopkins University Press, Lippincott/Harper, *New England Journal of Medicine*, VCH, MIT Press Journals, Elsevier (Netherlands), Pergamon Press (Oxford), The American Mathematical Society, Cambridge University Press, and Alan R. Liss.

    6. Twenty-three pioneers representing various segments within the computer industry offer their personal projections on the future of personal computing. See Ken Greenberg, ed., "The Shape of Things to Come," *PC World*, January 1986:143-151.

    7. *Information Please Almanac* (Boston: Houghton Mifflin Company, 1986), p. 145.

    8. Two such price studies are: Rebecca T. Lenzini, "Periodicals Prices-1983-1985 Update," *The Serials Librarian*, 9, no. 4 (Summer 1985):119-130; and Judith G. Horn, "Library Materials Price Index," *RTSD Newsletter*, 10, no. 2 (1985):19-20.

    9. Rebecca Lenzini and Judith Horn, "1977-1985: Formulative Years for the Subscription Agency," *The Serials Librarian*, 10, nos. 1/2 (Fall 1985/Winter 1986):225-238.

    10. Ibid., p. 225.

    11. Ibid., p. 234.

    12. See Charles Hamaker and Deana Astle, "Recent Pricing Patterns in British Journal Publishers," *Library Acquisitions Practice and Theory*, 8 (1984):7-14.

    13. Jan Derthick, School of Library Science, University of North Carolina, Chapel Hill, conducted recently "A Study of Serial Agent Selection Among the University Members of the Association of Research Libraries."

    14. Marcia Tuttle, "Magazine Fulfillment Centers: What They Are, How They Operate, and What We Can Do About Them," *Library Acquisitions: Practice and Theory*, 9, 1985:41-49.

    15. "Fulfillment Houses," *FaxLetter*, 1, no. 6 (November/December 1985):1-2.

The Library's Cost and the Vendor's Price for Serials

James T. Stephens

The most amazing aspect of serials pricing is that the authors of the content sometimes pay the publisher to be published. So, for the most part, there is no cost for the raw information and knowledge prior to its processing and delivery to the user.

One of the main purposes of this volume, I assume, is to improve the return on investment as measured by the investment's valuation to the user. I assume, also, that the user is composed of the faculty and the students and that the library is the user's agent. I take the further position that the expenditure is the full cost to deliver the needed information in usable form and that procurement is the full process to deliver in usable form to the user.

Those persons in the business of information are entering an era where the package of printed paper will be challenged as the best medium for the dissemination of information. Since all pricing and costs with which we have experience are based on information disseminated and handled as a package of printed paper, we must know these costs in full detail and scope in order to compare with the alternative costs of electronic storage and dissemination of information. The facilities, systems, and costs of publishers, agencies, and libraries are based on information as a package of printed paper, and it is as yet unclear what facilities, systems, and costs need exist for information collected and disseminated electronically. The frontier of the evaluation of the printed paper package versus electronic storage and dissemination is in secondary publishing. Those who indexed and abstracted manuscripts to make more efficient use of the packages of printed paper have tried to maintain their economic status as usage has switched to online search and retrieval and as a major part of the revenue stream from their information has flowed to online information distributors. Publisher pricing of the right to disseminate information electronically when this might cause diminished subscription revenue has been confusing. An organization with costs built on information packaged as printed paper is tested to understand the shape of costs and the necessary pricing for survival if information is collected, stored and disseminated electronically. The best medium for delivering information in usable form to the user should and will win out. Proper understanding of costs is one component of the comparative evaluation at this time.

In considering the price of serials, the frustration of wide variations is somewhat soothed by recognition that serials are the essence of the opposite of a commodity. Most traditional purchasing systems are based on the premise that what is being bought is commodity-like and subject to comparison. Most information in manuscripts or articles is unique, and most issues of multiple articles are even more unique. The uniqueness has legal status by our copyright laws. Difference among serials, whether the same subject, the same volume of data and the same frequency of publication or not, is the norm and makes price judgments difficult. You deal in purchasing the unique. If the aim is to be complete, this leads to excess. If the aim is to price-compare, the challenge is formidable. It seems to me it is useful when a financial limit simply exists, and the judgment process is narrowed to what information do we want because it is the most valuable. The point of view that a certain percentage of the budget should be spent on serials or monographs has never seemed appropriate. How information is packaged should not be an issue in deciding what to buy. The money should be spent where the value is greatest. As the information is not a commodity, neither is the service by the subscription agent. Many libraries who have tried to save 1-3 percent of the total expenditure on the subscription agent's services have delayed and missed information for their users through failure to recognize the importance of the quality of the vehicle for ordering, claiming, and serials management services.

My third and last situational comment is to ask where is the potential for the buyer, the library, to get a better return in the exchange with the producers—the author, publisher and subscription agent? It seems to me an improvement in return is only marginally available from trying to influence the price levels set on the producer's side of the interaction. The best return from the cost of information can come to the library by improving the measurement of the quality of information purchased in order to save by rejecting the unsatisfactory. The best return for what is spent in servicing these acquisitions can come from less costly internal handling methods. Subscription agents can and should aid in lowering administrative costs. Librarians are typically of the education or service culture and many regrettably are uncomfortable with commercial negotiation and evaluation. The librarians need to recognize comfortably and factually that the commercial person and firm are out to advantage themselves as is the nature of competitive commerce but that this fully and completely includes helping the customer. The librarians need to approach their duties in dealing with vendors as a business person perhaps more than as a librarian.

LIBRARY COST CONSIDERATIONS

Let me address library cost considerations in dealing with serials. Cost has two components. The first is what the vendor is paid. The second is the internal cost of the library to procure and obtain delivery from the vendor. The library must be in a position to evaluate both. In evaluating its cost, the library must understand and judge the vendor's systems and procedures and the vendor's service responsiveness with which it must interact.

In evaluating library costs, one must quantify. In EBSCO, we use $16.00 per hour as the full cost of the average order handling and service handling employee's time. This is 26¢ per minute. In my judgment, the compensation and benefit level are probably less in most agencies than in most university libraries. In my judgment, there is too little library management looking at staff time as 30¢ per minute. Opportunities to save 30¢ minutes exist and should be sought and tested continuously.

Library costs must have a whole institution and not just a library budget outlook. Big and public organizations are typified by tight financial controls. The cost of serials procurement includes the cost to administrative units outside of the library such as the finance office. Occasionally, we find libraries uninterested in the cost of serials activities to administrative units outside of the library, and this is a mistake.

What systems and procedures shared by the library and the agent are candidates for review with 30¢ per clerical minute in mind? The administrative and clerical input to renewing might be a candidate for simplification and time and money saving. If assigning serials by faculty department for periodic review of value is a process, an agent can code serials in order to generate review lists with current pricing by faculty department. A through Z renewal list checking if for the purpose of determining if the agent lists a title which should not be listed should not be a worthwhile investment of time, and an understanding of the agent's procedures should provide the confidence for this view. The generation and follow-up of claims is a steady and important task and should be continuously evaluated to minimize the input of minutes. Many libraries still backlog on the hand typing of claims. Terminals at the check-in station can minimize the mechanics of claim generation. The posting of payments at annual invoicing time should be studied. Agents can provide invoice records on magnetic tape or floppy disk and downloading to a computerized record can save many hours. Where computerized serials control as a component of an integrated library system is utilized, a subscription agent should be able to interface in order to exchange data with the system and to receive claims and orders online. Internal time for prospective serials order research should be evaluated against the availability of outside help. A significant cost of serials is the internal methodology for dealing with procurement and delivery, and these methods are a product of what a library's agents can offer and the two wish to implement. Continued methods improvement and cost cutting should be sought.

The full cost of ordering serials direct has been evaluated by numerous organizations and ranges from $10.00 to $35.00, depending on the accountant and the system used. Order direct serials should be prime candidates for placement with an agent on termination when the full cost of handling is weighed.

In addition to a subscription agent's systems and procedures, the library must make the suggestive-objective judgment of responsiveness. Recently, I read of the importance of evaluating automated systems by their "elegance" as well as by their functional characteristics. "Elegance" was defined as the ease of training for use, the ease of the command structure, etc. Such "soft" or "elegance" characteristics of a vendor's work as promptness, courtesy, and clarity of communications are a truly important aspect of overall service for procurement and delivery. An unreturned phone call or a very slowly answered letter are a real cost to the library and its users. A lower vendor price for equal systems but inferior responsiveness can be the case of a lower price but a higher cost for the library. On the front end, a library should evaluate both agency systems and personnel closely, should visit the administrative unit with which they will work, and should check references thoroughly. On the back end, the library should be candid with management if expectations are unmet.

An aggressive attitude toward methods simplification and a full effort to engage a vendor's capabilities for reducing work can very often reduce a library's costs of serials.

PUBLISHER PRICING

The diversity of publisher pricing for serials reflects the diversity of the community of publishers. Publishing is international and impacted by different national operating costs and business expectations. Publishers are both profit seeking corporations and nonprofit membership organizations with educational purposes. Some publishers deliver reader communities with advertising value and set their price more to generate greater numbers to please advertisers than to get revenue from subscription sales. *Fortune* generates approximately $13.00 in advertising revenue per copy per issue distributed. Some publishers secure virtually all their subscribers and revenue from libraries. Other publishers dislike the small percentage of their circulation which goes to libraries because of the issue collecting intensity of libraries.

The economics of publishing are unique in their relatively high fixed versus variable costs. The fixed costs are those the publisher has regardless of the number of issues produced. When the concept of inter-library lending gathered momentum in the 1970s, it was destined to be less successful than hoped because of the fixed cost nature of publishing. The idea was to group and reduce subscriptions through lending. If fully successful, the situation would have forced most publishers to advance the price in direct proportion to the subscription reductions. Publishers will naturally fight to maintain their economic status. If a serial operates above the break-even point, most of the revenue from the increment of subscriptions above the break-even point goes to the bottom of the income statement as profitability. Therefore, while each reduced subscription might be a small percentage of the total circulation, it could have a substantive impact on net profit. A scientific journal publisher with 1200 subscriptions whose profit is composed of that 90 percent of the subscription price which is not variable on the 200 of the 1200 subscriptions which were sold after the break-even point was reached will lose 25 percent of profits with the drop of only 50 (or 4 percent) subscriptions. The profit dynamics up and down the scale are strong. If a new journal does not meet the required break-even, often a publisher will run up the price to test its viability and let it lapse if the market says no.

I think a question librarians have with serials subscription prices is whether such is "fair." If so, such a question is probably not relevant. If a publisher can get profitable, there are simply too many standards and viewpoints to be constructive in addressing the question of fair profit and a fair price.

A recent issue dealing with fairness is, of course, U.S. subscription pricing by the community of British publishers. An article in 1984 (Hamaker, 1984) cited a survey of 548 British titles averaging a price higher in North America by 66 percent when compared with the U.K. price and by 34 percent when compared with the rest of the world. I have been told by at least one British publisher that discriminatory U.S. pricing is because the American market can afford it.

It is interesting to note that the community of publishers in this survey included the educator controlled university presses of the world's two oldest English-speaking universities and two companies also in the subscription agency business. In the last two years, North American librarians initiated an effort at moral persuasion. There will be impact, but it will not reduce prices in the U.S. The economics will not allow such. The U.S. probably represents 40 percent of the market for British publishers. If we assume an average of 40 percent premium in pricing over the actual cost of delivery, we have 16 percent of total publisher revenue associated with the discriminatory pricing to the U.S. market. It is improbable that many U.K. publishers exceed an overall 16 percent profit margin, so probably their entire profitability stems from this discriminatory pricing.

Therefore, assuming they are not willing to lower their profits, the alternative which might satisfy North American librarians and diminish the communications is to raise the overseas prices. We see signs of this occurring.

What is a fair price for a serial? With the assumption that a page of text is a good unit of measurement for the price of serials, but with the understanding that a final judgment requires also a qualitative evaluation of the text, a little sampling clearly indicates enormously wide variation. A range of 9¢ per page of text to $1.30 per page of text emerged from a small sampling recently done by me. A journal in the humanities from a university press and a journal of surgery from a society had a price of 9¢ per page of text. A library journal published by a librarian and one from a successful commercial publishing company were respectively 11¢ and 25¢ per page of text. A European journal of engineering was 21¢ per page, while a British engineering journal was 25¢ per page. Two non-newsstand business journals published in Britain by a company owned by university educators were $1.28 and $1.30 per page of text.

What is information worth? It is probably not constructive to debate the answer. Evaluation of the expenditure for that information packaged as a serial requires practical and objective measurements as well as qualitative judgment. Quantity of use and price per page of text are two variables with which faculty and library should be able to work in determining value in order to save or reallocate funds. Top library management should question what percentage of the information budget is justified for operating the mechanics of measurement and the machinery of evaluation in order to manage the expenditure for the most appropriate return.

SUBSCRIPTION AGENCY PRICING

The subscription agency's two most directly variable costs are the subscription agency cost of the subscriptions and the financing costs. While not typically thought to be the case, the cost of each can vary substantially among libraries of the same type. It is not unusual for two similar universities to have a meaningful difference in the margin of profit between the cumulative publishers' retail and the cumulative costs from the publisher to the agent. Typically, the service load imposed by a library is not well measured on an individual basis and is not much of a factor in the setting of price. It seems to me consideration of this factor will increase in the future. The inefficient library can indeed cost the agency relatively more at the 25¢ to 30¢ per minute which it costs to do business.

There are two interesting issues dealing with the handling charge in connection with agency pricing. The handling charge arose in the U.S. in the early 1960s with some publishers eliminating the traditional agency discount. The American Medical Association was the first to do so. Over the years, other publishers have eliminated or reduced the agency discount. A narrowing margin of profit forced agencies to adopt a handling or service charge. Publisher reasons for discount reduction or elimination vary. Some say they cannot afford the discount to agencies. Some say the agencies serve the library primarily, and the library should pay. On the question of the publisher not being able to afford the discount, agencies in wanting to service libraries fully for the library's convenience have done a poor job of putting publishers to the test of what they can afford by letting them handle library subscriptions direct. Undoubtedly, the benefits of agencies providing sales and advertising help, a common order format, payment up front, and buffering many communications save publishers considerably. On the question of whether the subscription agency serves the library or the publisher primarily, the agency serves both. To argue the question is to evade and excuse for it is an eternally debatable topic. The electronic transmission of data between agencies and publishers is rapidly increasing. Such constitutes significant benefit for the publisher. I expect to see a tightening of attitude by subscription agencies with respect to their willingness to tolerate and service those publishers who do not provide a reasonable trade discount.

How the handling charge is invoiced is relevant. The world is split with North America traditionally invoicing the handling charge at the bottom of the invoice as a separate line item and the rest of the world invoicing the handling charge in the line item. One of the ironies of price pressure for North American subscription agencies in that librarians do like to talk price is our knowledge of the traditionally much better profit margins enjoyed by overseas agents. These are often enjoyed in the servicing of U.S. libraries who historically have not put forth the effort to understand the handling charge from the overseas agent. It has been frustrating to see margins narrow for U.S. agents while many North American libraries pay significantly higher handling charges to foreign agents and demonstrate reluctance to place non-U.S. serials with American agencies who often have the same overseas capabilities as the foreign agents. The line item pricing of the handling charge can be communicated as a total for comparative pricing. It probably provides the most logical method because of the no-discount publishers. Currently, North American libraries with the handling charge at the bottom of the invoice do not know the true cost of the library of those serials which provide the agent no discount and thereby make mandatory the handling charge. In recent years, a major nonprofit publisher in the U.S. with most subscriptions from libraries via subscription agencies chose to eliminate the agency discount to get more revenue invisibly and without a price increase for fear of losing subscriptions. It is increasingly an untenable situation which possibly calls for loading the handling charge to those titles which cause it. The total price to the library would not change, but the true cost per title would be known.

SUMMARY

In the long term, how does the library get the best buy? With respect to the cost of information in packages of printed paper, I suggest a checking of text page cost and usage data should be coupled with the qualitative appraisal of the material by faculty and library staff in order simply to judge value against the availability of money and the alternatives for its use. With respect to vendor cost, the exploration should be as one business person to another business person. Vendor systems and procedures should be evaluated for their ability to save library costs. Vendor responsiveness should be continuously judged and tested. Libraries should view their cost of serials as inclusive of the cost of their procedures and systems at probably 30¢ per minute and continually be evaluating all alternatives in seeking the best return possible.

REFERENCE

Charles Hamaker, "Recent Pricing Patterns in British Journal Publishing," *Library Acquisitions: Practice and Theory*, 8, 4 (1984):225-232.

Materials Costs and Collection Development in Academic Libraries

Lenore Clark

The function of collection development is to identify the current and future resource needs of the library's community and implement programs to satisfy those needs. How effectively a library fulfills this function depends on a number of factors—institutional, professional, social, political, demographic, technological, and financial. Financial conditions, particularly the price of books and serials, the number of books and serials published annually, and the funds available for purchasing them, are perhaps the most visible of these. And financial conditions have not been good. The facts have been amply documented, but to summarize: more than 70,000 books and 69,000 periodical titles were published last year. These numbers are projected to increase annually, periodicals by an estimated 1.6 to 7.6 percent. The hardcover book which cost $8.77 in 1969 cost $30.00 in 1984, and the journal which cost $8.66 in 1969 cost $54.97 in 1984.[1] These figures do not reflect the hundreds of thousands of unpublished scholarly works which appear annually.

Over a similar period, increases in academic library support from federal, state, and private sources declined while demands on the library increased: a rapid growth in knowledge and new doctoral programs generated a need for more scholarly materials; enrollments, though down, brought diverse student bodies with even more diverse resource needs; new and different forms of information are expected to be in libraries, along with expanded services; rapidly advancing technology has accelerated demand for physical as well as bibliographic access; legislators and administrators, themselves beset by increased demands and reduced revenues, insist on greater accountability. One cannot discuss materials costs and collection development outside this context of contracted and strained library funding.

Taking into account these internal and external pressures, this paper will examine how price and cost fluctuations affect collection development and how collection development programs and activities respond.

Let us begin by looking at the best case: slowed inflation, a strengthened dollar abroad, and/or improved library funding. This past year a strengthened dollar meant American libraries could purchase European

© 1987 by The Haworth Press, Inc. All rights reserved.

monographs and serials more cheaply, except where publishers established artificially high U.S. dollar rates, and inflation in monograph and serials prices has slowed. What should be noted, however, is that although the rate of inflation has decreased, prices continue to increase; and even hefty increments in library materials budgets are no longer sufficient to keep pace with the compound demands of rising prices and the annual increase in scholarly output. To illustrate, between 1974 and 1984 ARL libraries' monographs and other nonserial materials expenditures increased by 93 percent and current serials expenditures increased by 155 percent while the number of volumes added increased by only 31 percent.[1]

A wide range of interrelated collection development responses have been devised or are evolving to cope with these financial stringencies. For the sake of discussion I describe these separately as the six "C"s: Compensating, Cost-Cutting, Communication, Consumerism, Collection Management, and Coordinated Collection Development.

COMPENSATING

Compensating is characterized by relative passivity toward cost fluctuations, often with greater reliance on improved funding to offset price increases.

Shifting funds from the monographs budget to the serials budget is a common form of compensating. Libraries shift monographs funds to serials in order to protect vital research support and sometimes also to avoid cancellation decisions which would be unpopular with faculty. Herbert White predicted in 1979 that if the budgetary shift continued at the same rate as had been observed in his study, major academic libraries would be buying no new monographs in 1990.[2]

Some libraries appear to be fairly detached from the economic problems of materials inflation and price discrimination. As recently as 1984, Ruschin and others expressed amazement at librarians' lack of concern about discriminatory pricing of foreign periodicals in the United States.[3] Certainly, large, well-funded libraries can absorb higher prices with less pain than smaller libraries, even though it is the large research collections which are affected most directly dollarwise. But there also appears to be a reluctance on the part of some to participate in collective action which might obligate them to cancel important journals or curtail purchases of needed resources.

Even with tight economic conditions, it appears that price alone does not influence selection and renewal decisions to a significant extent. The majority of responses to a survey of selection practices among academic, special and large public libraries conducted for the Association of American Publishers in 1984 indicated that price and special offer discounts influenced librarians' selection decisions only Sometimes, rather than Always or Frequently or Never.[4] These findings are supported by the Conoco Study survey currently being conducted by the Research Libraries Group Collection Management and Development Committee, in which bibliographers were queried about selection of specific titles in their fields. Thus far in response to the question, "If this title is not owned, why was it not acquired?", "too expensive" was cited as the reason in only three-tenths of 1 percent (0.3) of the answers (18 out of nearly 6,000 occurrences).* Here too, it should be noted that the majority of RLG members are large research libraries.

To obtain a sense of how academic libraries around the country are coping with economic pressures, fifteen university libraries ranging from large ARL libraries to smaller institutions were surveyed informally by telephone during the months of November and December 1985. Three of the medium-sized libraries had recently received major one-time grants either from special state appropriations or from fund-raising drives; four others had been allocated substantial budget increases following several years of decline. In none of these seven libraries was funding provided for additional staff to process materials. The general effect of austerity level staffing coupled with sudden increases in book money was a lessened concern for discounts and price and an emphasis on speedy, hassle-free fulfillment which would not bog down personnel. This is a trade-off that collection librarians are pressed into because of continuing stringent budgets or lack of understanding on the part of funding bodies.

Compensating for rising costs by obtaining increased support is a high priority for every library director. Principal strategies to influence the funding side of the price/publication/budget equation include lobbying administrators, legislators, and other governing bodies, and establishing more aggressive gift and donor programs.

COST-CUTTING

Nancy Gwinn and Warren Haas point out, "the academic library cannot use cost-cutting methods available to other institutional components and continue to carry out its role. It cannot reduce its collection or services as a university can reduce the number of sections of a course or close dormitories and cafeterias. Whether the campus population increases or declines the library must continue to acquire the books, jour-

---

*Jim Coleman, 3 February 1986, personal communication.

nals, and other materials that serve the educational and research programs."[5]

However, cost-cutting must and does take place. Depending on the financial condition of the library and its institutional outlook, responses vary from crisis-impelled measures, such as aborting approval plans or stopping all book purchases mid-year, to more proactive planning for gradual contraction. Some of the deliberate accommodations libraries make to these pressures are:[6]

a. Reduce foreign purchases.
b. Delay or reduce retrospective purchases.
c. Limit the purchase of multiple copies of books.
d. Freeze journal subscriptions and initiate new subscriptions only if subscriptions of an equivalent dollar amount are cancelled.
e. Eliminate duplicate subscriptions.
f. Cancel single-copy subscriptions.
g. Encourage faculty members to donate review copies of books and personal subscriptions to the library and ask new journal editors on campus to donate a free subscription to their journal and review copies on a regular basis.
h. Increase exchange programs.
i. Purchase paperbacks in lieu of hardcover books.
j. Emphasize government documents as possible substitutes for new trade publications.
k. Substitute microform, electronic, or other noncodex formats where they are more cost-effective.
l. Cancel indexing and abstracting services and substitute online services.
m. Charge the user for these online services.
n. Postpone purchase of new editions of reference works.
o. Seek higher discounts from vendors or purchase books from specialized discount stores.
p. Purchase monographs and serials from the country of original publication.
q. Place increased reliance on approval plans to assure a steady flow of current imprints and to save technical services processing costs.
r. Reduce or cancel approval plans.
s. Cancel monographic series standing orders and all-publications plans and select on a title-by-title basis.

These and other cost-cutting measures are varyingly effective, although some tend to be short-term, short-sighted adjustments, and the savings many of them generate are relatively insignificant. Insofar as they improve efficiency and streamline procedures they can result in lasting economies.

The following represent more basic and long-range approaches to the problem:

COMMUNICATION

More than ever, significant communication must occur between libraries and their governing bodies, their constituents, their suppliers, and other libraries for the purpose of educating, lobbying, sharing information, and promoting cooperation.

Library-Governing Bodies Communication

The library director today must not only be a skilled manager, she or he must also be an effective lobbyist and publicist, able to persuade the legislature and the academic administration of the library's vital importance to higher education and its need for a larger share of the budget. The director must also be able to elucidate more concretely than in the past the severity of the predicament libraries face and indicate the rational courses of action, including the necessity for planned contraction.

Director-Staff Communication

Even though the literature is filled with documented concerns about problems of inflation and no-growth budgets, many librarians continue to expect institutions to accord the same importance to their needs as they themselves do. The library administrator must educate members of the library staff about economic pressures and the consequent stringencies, and guide them to accept realistically revised priorities and goals.

Librarian-Librarian Communication

Increasingly collection development librarians share information about collections, spread the word about publishers and vendors, exchange strategies for improved programs and procedures, and otherwise behave cooperatively through informal contact and through professional organizations.

Library-Academic Community Communication

If faculty are the library's most articulate supporters, they are at the same time the most antagonistic when curtailments in purchasing are proposed. Professors continue to expect on-site access to journals and monographs in their field, and suggestions of interinstitutional borrowing, even of highly specialized, expensive journals, often meet with recalcitrance, although to a lesser degree today than ten years ago. Their wariness about journal use studies is well known. Too often, a faculty member's political profile, rather than merit or use, determines selection and cancellation choices. Regular meetings between faculty and library liaisons, one-on-one contact, inclusion of faculty members on library committees, and wide distribution of library news and information, including current problems associated with costs, are some of the ways libraries try to gain faculty understanding and support for reduced purchasing.

Improved document delivery is a high priority for most libraries, and progress has been good. But this is another area where faculty must be educated to accept the fact that borrowing of lesser-used materials is necessary and some inconvenience will be unavoidable until the time instant retrieval is achieved.

CONSUMERISM

Communication between librarians and publishers has assumed greater weight as a direct result of fifteen years of unabating inflation, and, more recently, as a result of discriminatory pricing by certain European publishers. Not surprisingly, much of the communication has been adversarial. What is significant, however, is the consumerist dimension this communication has assumed and its demonstrated potential as an adjunct to collection management.

Spreading the Word Through Publication

Libraries' complaints about pricing had been generally ineffectual, at least until recently, when articles and letters began to appear with increasing frequency documenting inflation and price discrimination; accusing publishers of price gouging, publishing too many journals—particularly in paper format—deliberately increasing volume output, publishing inefficiently, and impeding the free flow of information; and exhorting libraries to cancel or boycott overpriced journals. Especially since Richard DeGennaro's 1977 call to "fight back"[7] and several subsequent letters and articles by others[8,9,10,11,12,13,3,14,15] have librarians' concerns been confirmed, their indignation articulated and the collective consciousness raised. At the same time, the issue of pricing has become intensely newsworthy, which has brought media reinforcement. Paul and Ruschin both note how American libraries took an activist stance against discriminatory pricing by certain German publishers in the 1930s. But consumerism did not exist as a movement in the thirties and the outcry subsided once the issue was resolved. Today, the reach of communication is far greater and consumerism has become a pervasive force in American society, which suggests a continuing and significant role for library consumerism.

Exerting Pressure Through Professional Organizations

Professional organizations have also mobilized. The American Library Association and the Association of Research Libraries, for example, have underscored the issue of discriminatory pricing through meetings, committee investigations, published resolutions, delegations to publishers and booksellers, and indirect threats of sanctions and legal action.[16] And newsletters and journals of special and regional library groups regularly carry alerts about discriminatory pricing and other objectionable practices. That activism has been directly responsible for the recently slowed rate of inflation or the reduced differential between European and American subscription prices cannot be documented; however, it is not unreasonable to assume some causal connection. The international seminar on British journal pricing held in London in March 1985 was noteworthy not only for its content but for the inclusion of an ALA representative on its program. Had U.S. libraries not applied pressure, they probably would not have been invited to state their position in a forum of this kind. Marcia Tuttle, who spoke at the seminar as ALA delegate, commented in her report, "Now that the practice (discriminatory pricing) has been publicized and criticized, almost certainly something will be done. It will not be as much or as soon as we would like, but it will be at least a gesture. . . . Several librarians are studying these prices, and their watchfulness will help persuade the publishers to continue to bring prices into line."[17] On the other hand, evidence that discriminatory pricing practices may be spreading to certain publishers in Germany and other European countries suggests that American library consumerism has not been sufficiently daunting. In a recent report to the joint meeting of the Chief Collection Development Officers of Large Research Libraries Discussion Group and Chief Collection Development Officers of Medium-Sized Research Libraries Discussion Group, Robert Miller, Chair of the ARL Collection Development Committee, commented that the committee had been buoyed by an improvement in the discriminatory pricing situation in Great Britain. "But now it appears to be spreading. It appears that unless we take away dollars where our mouth is, we are not going to get a lot done."[18] In his definition of "consumerism," Robert Heller, author of the *Pocket Manager,* notes, "In the present . . . and in the future, manufacturers can never forget that an adverse consumerist reaction may be poison. . . . The ancient doctrine of *caveat emptor* has gone out of the window: the new rule is *caveat vendor* — and the vendor had better not forget it."[19]

Promoting Dialogue Through Professional Organizations

The surge of librarian, publisher, and vendor participation in professional groups which are organized to exchange information about resources, talk over grievances, and promote regular communication is one of the more sanguine aspects of the concern about pricing and costs since the 1970s.

COLLECTION MANAGEMENT

Thus far the discussion has centered on how inflation and discriminatory pricing is affecting libraries and the ways in which libraries are responding, on the one hand, by economizing and compensating for rising costs and, on the other, by influencing pricing. The most significant response, however, has been philosophical. Reflected in the more recent emphasis on the term "collection *management*," it assumes that even if a greater share of available monies are channeled into libraries, which they undoubtedly ought to be, libraries cannot realistically expect to keep pace with rising prices and increasing scholarly output. It assumes that the situation is not likely to be reversed in the foreseeable future. It recognizes that the old goal of building comprehensive research collections, or even of building balanced collections, has been invalidated, superseded by a limited growth concept which emphasizes access over ownership, client-centered collections, and effective working collections. It accepts the notion of "The Library," the aggregation of the holdings of all libraries, rather than self-sufficient local collections, and it emphasizes efficient, timely access to needed information wherever and in whatever format it may be. "Order, Acquisition, Collection Development, Collection Management — the names are interesting in themselves, borrowed in fact from other disciplines, but their implications are greater. They represent a shift from external to internal control, from passivity to action."[20] The fact is, the enormous growth in the importance of collection management and development as a field of librarianship is the direct outcome of the economic pressures which have afflicted libraries for the past fifteen years.

Management Information

The "reconceptualization of collection development,"[21] as Charles Osburn terms it, places greater reliance than ever before on precise, standardized information, planning, and sharing of resources.

Accountability and collection effectiveness have become paramount concerns. Is the library making the best use of each dollar spent on books and periodicals? To what extent are patrons' immediate resource needs being satisfied? How much of what is purchased is needed locally? How large should the local library collection be? How will future resource needs be met? To facilitate positive responses, collection management programs seek to identify patrons' needs, describe existing collection strengths and current collecting intensities, and activate plans to bring resources into closer alignment with those needs. Increasingly, through title and volume counts, bibliography and citation checks, and other measuring techniques, libraries assemble qualitative and quantitative data which describe the contents and character of collections. By recording these data in detailed, uniform subject categories and measuring them against increasingly objective external benchmarks and standards, relative strengths and weaknesses are identified. By measuring them against teaching and research needs and monitoring their use, their effectiveness is further assessed and informed access and relegation decisions are made. Comparisons within and between institutions, documented through an increasingly common language, add dimension and validity to evaluations. The National Shelflist Count project, which in 1973 involved seventeen libraries and in 1985 included forty-eight, allows for quantitative comparisons in 490 standard LC classifications. The Research Libraries Group conspectus and verification studies, recently adopted by ARL for the North American Collections Inventory Project, facilitates comparative description and assessment in some 5,000 subjects. And other methodologies are being developed to assist libraries in defining and communicating collecting goals.

The Conoco Project, a pilot study in progress in selected RLG libraries, may produce the most concrete information yet about equations between cost and collection development. In his instructions to study participants, Scott Bennett explained, ". . . existing collections represent decades of capital investment and are, cumulatively, not susceptible to much change. . . . If we want to make changes that foster cooperative management of our collections, the place to do it is in our current collecting practices. . . . The Conoco study is an attempt to document these practices. . . ."[22] Conoco surveys distributed to seventeen RLG bibliographers in Geology and German Studies asked eight questions relating to specific selection decisions in their field. Responses to the coded questions are expected to yield objective data about the nature and anatomy of collecting practices, including the cost of building and maintaining collections at specific support levels.

Accounting and price data have also been restructured over the past ten years to yield fiscal information which corresponds more directly with academic subject categories. Collated and analyzed to assess current support of collections and project future expenditure patterns, they provide the basis of the carefully formulated budget request, which is an essential component of sound collection management.

Automation has made it possible for libraries to obtain and share enormous quantities of information about collection content, collection growth, use, and costs via a wide range of access points. Local microcomputers and turnkey systems and computerized vendor reports and services, the national OCLC and RLIN utilities, the RLG online conspectus, the AMIGOS Collection Analysis Services, and countless other electronic programs provide management data which would be unobtainable manually.

Control and Planning

In contrast to the freewheeling expansionism of the sixties when libraries confidently expected to purchase most of the monographs and serials their constituents requested, the emphasis since the mid-seventies has been on planning for controlled growth or contraction and on adaptability to programmatic and budgetary shifts and changing economic conditions. The principal long-range planning instrument is the collection development policy which describes the library's collection intensities and collecting aims and details its plans for future resource support in each area. A flexible document, it is intended to be amenable to periodic revision to assure responsiveness to changing conditions.

Collection development librarians, in close consultation with the academic community, are assuming primary responsibility for positive and negative decisions concerning selection and access. Collection reviews are undertaken with greater attention to other cost factors besides materials, such as staffing, space, bindery budgets, alternative access, and long-range preservation needs. And to assure responsiveness and flexibility, existing commitments and procedures are regularly re-evaluated to assess cost-effectiveness, relevance to academic programs, and relative importance to local patrons.

There is an increased focus on preservation and disaster preparedness programs. Preservation activities are expensive, but maintaining libraries' resources is not only economical over the long-term, it is imperative if the world's recorded scholarship is to be safeguarded.

Higher costs, more titles to choose from, limited funds with which to purchase them, and complex preservation and access choices, make it more difficult and costly than ever to make wise collection decisions. For this reason, the training of collection development librarians is also stressed.

COORDINATED COLLECTION DEVELOPMENT

Whether voluntarily or involuntarily, libraries are reducing acquisitions, and in an effort to lessen the burden of extensively duplicated book purchases and costly research collections and to concentrate funds on strong local collections, they and their governing bodies are, with increasing purposefulness, seeking ways to implement coordinated collection arrangements. For the more immediately impacted small and medium-sized academic libraries, coordinated collection development offers assurance that retrenchment will not mean the loss of research resources. For the more affluent libraries, coordinated collection development ensures that the widespread decisions which inflation and diminished budgets have necessitated will not lead to attrition of entire areas of research support. The pace at which individual libraries adjust their local collecting practices to participate actively in coordinated collection development programs is uncertain, since each institution must establish a satisfactory balance between economy and service. What is unarguable, however, is the inevitability of interinstitutional dependence and the necessity for coordinated planning. Here, too, communication and sound collection management information are at the heart of a successful coordinated effort—communication with the academic community to gain their cooperation, and communication between libraries to exchange reliable collection data through the vehicle of a common language.

Even if large libraries need not be as constrained about purchasing costly monographs and serials, their leadership in establishing national collection development and preservation programs reflects their recognition of the urgent need for shared responsibility for acquisition and management of the world's scholarship. The RLG Conspectus and ARL's North American Collections Inventory Project facilitate cooperation on a continental scale by mapping existing collection strengths and current collecting intensities through the use of a standardized collection description instrument. However, there are more than 366 local, regional and national consortial arrangements in the United States and Canada in various stages of implementation which approach cooperation from a variety of directions; for example, North Carolina's relatively homogeneous, highly successful fifty-five-year-old Triangle Research Libraries Network; the significant five-state multi-type Library and Information Resources in the Pacific Northwest (LIRN) Project, not yet fully implemented, and the major national resource sharing consortium, the Center for Research Libraries.

In his report to the joint Chief Collection Development Officers of Large Research and the Medium-Sized Research Libraries at the American Library Association midwinter conference, John Finzi, Director of

Collection Development at the Library of Congress, discussed major cuts—recent and impending—in the Library of Congress budget. He ended with the admonition that cooperative programs will have to become very substantial.[23]

CONCLUSION

Even the best planned collection management and development programs cannot operate successfully under prolonged and extreme conditions of financial stress. William Dix, looking at budget cutting as early as 1971, commented, "We shall obviously have to practice more austerity, but at what point does austerity on top of austerity produce emaciation and anemia?"[24] The financial adversities of high prices, overpublication, broadened mission and constricted resources over the past fifteen years have yielded certain beneficial effects, however: libraries have achieved more productive working relations with one another; the library profession has gained in cohesion; unessential commitments and useless materials are being eliminated from collections and indiscriminate purchasing practices are under better control; libraries are learning a great deal more about their collections and those of others and they are learning how to manage them more prudently; budgeting methods have been sharpened; communication between all sectors of the information community—publishers, bookdealers, libraries, and the patron—has been expanded. Planned collection management strategies are gradually being put into place to deal positively with the financial uncertainties. In the meantime, libraries continue to cope according to the six Cs, hopefully with increasing emphasis on communication, consumerism, collection management, and coordinated collection development.

NOTES

1. Statistical sources: *Bowker Annual of Book & Trade Information 1972.* New York: R.R. Bowker, 1972; *Bowker Annual of Library & Book Trade Information.* New York: R.R. Bowker, 1985; Grannis, Chandler B., "Title Output and Average Prices; 1984 Final Figure." *Publishers Weekly* 28 (August 23,1985):43; *UNESCO Statistical Yearbook 1984.* Paris: United Nations Educational, Scientific and Cultural Organization, 1984; *ARL Statistics 1983-1984.* Washington, DC: Association of Research Libraries, 1985; Harvey, John F., and Spyers-Duran, Peter, "The Effect of Inflation on Academic Libraries." In *Austerity Management in Academic Libraries,* edited by John F. Harvey and Peter Spyers-Duran, pp. 1-42. Metuchen, NJ: Scarecrow Press, 1984; Taylor, David C., *Managing the Serials Explosion.* New York: Knowledge Industries, 1982; *Ulrich's International Periodicals Directory.* New York: R.R. Bowker, 1985.

2. White, Herbert S., "Library Materials Prices and Academic Library Practices: Between Scylla and Charybdis." *The Journal of Academic Librarianship* 5 (1979):20-23.

3. Ruschin, Siegfried, "Why Are Foreign Subscription Rates Higher for American Libraries Than They Are for Subscribers Elsewhere?" *The Serials Librarian* 9 (Spring 1985):7-17.

4. Center for Book Research, University of Scranton, *Library Acquisitions Survey.* New York: The Association of American Publishers, Inc., 1985.

5. Gwinn, Nancy E., and Haas, Warren J., "Crisis in the College Library." *AGB Reports*, March/April 1981, pp. 14-45.

6. Sources consulted in addition to references cited elsewhere: Reid, Marion T., "Coping with Budget Adversity: The Impact of the Financial Squeeze on Acquisitions." *College & Research Libraries* 37 (May 1976):266- 272; Burton, Robert E., "Book Selection and Budget Cuts in Academic Libraries." *Michigan Librarian* 41 (1975):7-9; Johnson, Steve, "Serials Deselection in University Libraries: The Next Step." *Library Acquisitions: Practice and Theory* 7 (1983):239-246; Varma, D. K., "Increasing Subscription Costs and Problems of Resource Allocation." *Special Libraries* 74 (January 1983):61-66.

7. DeGennaro, Richard, "Escalating Journal Prices: Time to Fight Back." *American Libraries* 8 (February 1977):69-74.

8. Kronenfeld, Michael R., and Thompson, James A., "The Impact of Inflation on Journal Costs." *Library Journal* 106 (April 1, 1981):714-717.

9. Dyl, Edward A., "A Note on Price Discrimination by Academic Journals." *Library Quarterly* 53 (May 1983):161-168.

10. Besant, Larry X., and Ruschin, Siegfried, "Price of European Journals." *Nature* 310 (August 2, 1984):358.

11. Hamaker, Charles, and Astle, Deana A., "Recent Pricing Patterns in British Journal Publishing." *Library Acquisitions: Practicing and Theory* 8 (1984):225-232.

12. Paul, Huibert, "Serials: Higher Prices vs. Shrinking Budgets." *The Serials Librarian* 9 (Winter 1984):3-12.

13. Hale, Charles E., "Library Consumerism: A Need for Concerted Action." *Technicalities* 4 (May 1984):8-9.

14. Joyce, Patrick, and Merz, Thomas E., "Price Discrimination in Academic Journals." *Library Quarterly* 55 (July 1985):273-283.

15. Tuttle, Marcia, "The Pricing of British Journals for the North American Market." *Library Resources & Technical Services* 30 (January/March 1986):72-78.

16. "Foreign Journal Prices." *Association of Research Libraries Newsletter* no. 126 (July 26,1985), p. 3.

17. Tuttle, p. 77.

18. Miller, Robert C., Report to Joint Meeting of Chief Collection Development Officers of Large Research Libraries Discussion Group and Chief Collection Development Officers of Medium-Sized Research Libraries Discussion Group, 18 January 1986, at American Library Association Conference, Chicago.

19. Heller, Robert, *The Pocket Manager*. New York: E. P. Dutton, Inc., 1985, p. 51.

20. Martin, Murray S., "A Future for Collection Management." *Collection Management* 6 (Fall/Winter 1984):1.

21. Osburn, Charles B., "New Directions in Collection Development." *Technicalities* 2 (February, 1982):1, 3-4.

22. Bennett, Scott, Memorandum to Conoco Study Participants (3 July 1985).

23. Finzi, John, Report to Joint Meeting of Chief Collection Development Officers of Large Research Libraries Discussion Group and Chief Collection Development Officers of Medium-Sized Research Libraries Discussion Group, 18 January 1986, at American Library Association Conference, Chicago.

24. Dix, William S., "Reflections in Adversity; or, How Do You Cut a Library Budget?" *Library Lectures*, nos. 17-20 (January 1971–March 1972), p. 9.

For Product Safety Concerns and Information please contact our EU
representative GPSR@taylorandfrancis.com
Taylor & Francis Verlag GmbH, Kaufingerstraße 24, 80331 München, Germany

www.ingramcontent.com/pod-product-compliance
Lightning Source LLC
Chambersburg PA
CBHW052133300426
44116CB00010B/1879